HANDBOOK OF CONFEDERATE SWORDS

by
William A. Albaugh, III

Foreword by
Richard D. Steuart

THE CONFEDERATE
REPRINT COMPANY
☆ ☆ ☆ ☆
WWW.CONFEDERATEREPRINT.COM

Handbook of Confederate Swords
by William A. Albaugh, III

Originally Published in 1951
by Pioneer Press
Harriman, Tennessee

Reprint Edition © 2016
The Confederate Reprint Company
Post Office Box 2027
Toccoa, Georgia 30577
www.confederatereprint.com

Cover and Interior by
Magnolia Graphic Design
www.magnoliagraphicdesign.com

ISBN-13: 978-1945848001
ISBN-10: 1945848006

TABLE OF CONTENTS
☆ ☆ ☆ ☆

PREFACE 5

FOREWORD 7

ONE 23
    The Sword of Gen. Robert E. Lee

TWO 25
    James Conning – Mobile, Ala.

THREE 29
    Tallassee, Ala.

FOUR 31
    L. Haiman & Bro., Columbus, Ga.

FIVE 33
    L. Haiman & Bro., continued

SIX 37
    Macon, Ga., E.J. Johnston & Co., W.J. McElroy

SEVEN 41
    Thomas, Griswold & Co., New Orleans, La.

EIGHT 43
    Thomas, Griswold & Co., continued

NINE 47
    Thomas, Griswold & Co., continued

TEN 49
    Thomas, Griswold & Co., continued

ELEVEN 51
    Fayetteville, N.C.

4   HANDBOOK OF CONFEDERATE SWORDS

TWELVE 55
    Louis Froelich, Kernersville, N.C.

THIRTEEN. 57
    Kraft, Goldschmidt & Kraft, Columbia, S.C.

FOURTEEN 61
    Kraft, Goldschmidt & Kraft, continued

FIFTEEN 63
    Columbia, S.C.

SIXTEEN 65
    Gen. Wade Hampton's Sword

SEVENTEEN 69
    Nashville Plow Works, Nashville, Tenn.

EIGHTEEN 71
    L.T. Cunningham, College Hill Arsenal, Nashville, Tn.

NINETEEN 75
    Memphis Novelty Works, Thos. Leech & Co., Memphis

TWENTY. 77
    Memphis Novelty Works, continued

TWENTY-ONE 81
    Boyle Gamble & MacFee, Richmond, Va.

TWENTY-TWO 83
    Boyle Gamble & MacFee, continued

TWENTY-THREE 85
    Boyle Gamble & MacFee, continued

TWENTY-FOUR 87
    Boyle Gamble & MacFee, continued

TWENTY-FIVE 89
    Confederate Naval Cutlass

TWENTY-SIX 91
    Tredegar Iron Works, Richmond, Va.

TWENTY-SEVEN 93
    Tredegar Iron Works, continued
TWENTY-EIGHT 95
    Virginia Armory, Richmond, Va.
TWENTY-NINE 97
    Virginia Manufactory Sabres, Richmond, Va.
THIRTY 99
    Confederate Foot Officer's Sword
THIRTY-ONE 103
    Confederate Foot Officer's Sword, continued
THIRTY-TWO 105
    Confederate Field-Officers Sword
THIRTY-THREE 107
    Confederate Artillery (?) Sword
THIRTY-FOUR 109
    Confederate Short Sword
THIRTY-FIVE 111
    Short Artillery Sword (Foot)
THIRTY-SIX 115
    Short Artillery Sword (Foot)
THIRTY-SEVEN 117
    Confederate Naval Cutlass
THIRTY-EIGHT 119
    Robert Mole & Sons, Birmingham, England
THIRTY-NINE 123
    Robert Mole & Sons, continued
FORTY 125
    Robert Mole & Sons, continued
FORTY-ONE 127
    Robert Mole & Sons, continued

FORTY-TWO 127
    Isaac's & Co., London, England

FORTY-THREE 131
    S. Isaac's Campbell and Co., London, England

FORTY-FOUR 135
    German-Made Confederate Sword

FORTY-FIVE 137
    Unmarked Confederate Officer's Sword

FORTY-SIX 139
    Unmarked Confederate Officer's Sword

FORTY-SEVEN 141
    Confederate Cavalry Sabre

FORTY-EIGHT 143
    Unmarked Confederate Sabre

FORTY-NINE 145
    Unmarked Confederate Sabre

FIFTY 147
    Unmarked Confederate Sabre

FIFTY-ONE 149
    Unmarked Confederate Sabre

FIFTY-TWO 151
    Unmarked Confederate Sabre

FIFTY-THREE 153
    Unmarked Confederate Sabre

FIFTY-FOUR 155
    Unmarked Confederate Sabre

FIFTY-FIVE 157
    Unmarked Confederate Cavalry Sabre

FIFTY-SIX 159
    Homemade Confederate Sword

FIFTY-SEVEN 161
    "Homemade" Confederate Officer's Sword
FIFTY-EIGHT 163
    Confederate Naval Cutlass
FIFTY-NINE 165
    Swords of Confederate Manufacture in National Museum
SIXTY 167
    Swords Stamped "C.S.A."

PREFACE

Little has been written on the subject of Confederate swords, beyond a brief article which appeared in *The Confederate Veteran* of January 1926 by Richard D. Steuart, author of the foreword of the present work. Theodore T. Belote, in his bulletin No. 163, put out by the National Museum, describes several Confederate swords.

The short work which follows does not by any means describe all the types or manufacturers of swords for the Confederacy. It is not intended as a "history," but is only a pictorial and brief written description of those swords which we have seen during our years of collecting.

There are unquestionably many swords which we do not list, and of which we have not heard, but this little booklet may serve as a starting point for those that follow.

This volume is dedicated to the memory of John & Ira Albaugh of Maryland; my great-grandfather, and great-granduncle who served in the 1st Virginia Cavalry under Gen. J.E.B. Stuart, and who gave their lives for the Confederacy; one at Kelly's Ford, Va., in 1863, and the other at Bunker Hill, Va., in 1864.

Thanks is given to the gracious assistance of Miss India Thomas, and Miss Eleanor Brockenbrough, of the

Confederate Museum in Richmond, Va., in the permitting of access to the priceless relics in their custody.

FOREWORD
by Richard D. Steuart

*"Forth from its scabbard pure and bright,
Flashed the sword of Lee."* – Father Ryan

And thousands of other swords just as pure and bright if less expensive flashed in the Southern sunlight in the four years of warfare which marked what has been called the American Civil War, or the War between the States.

Poets may dream of the beauty of these stainless blades, drawn in a Lost Cause, but the matter of fact historian and collector would like to know whence came these swords?

The outbreak of the war in 1861, found stored in the Federal and State arsenals, thousands of old sabres, relics of the Revolutionary War, War of 1812, and Mexican War. They were clumsy, unwieldy weapons, with broad blades, heavy iron scabbards, wooden grips, and iron guards. Similar swords formed the armament of most of the various home militia companies throughout the South.

Also in private homes were many fine swords, relics of other wars, preserved as heirlooms, but of little use for actual service.

There were no sword factories in the South at the

beginning of the war. Swords had been manufactured at the Virginia Manufactory, or Richmond Armory, in the early years of the century, but apparently, their manufacture was discontinued about the time of the War of 1812.

Swords like dueling pistols, hunting rifles, and fowling pieces, Colt, and other revolvers were imported from Europe, or purchased from Northern Manufacturers by military outfitters in the South, such as Hyde & Goodrich, of New Orleans; Courtney & Tennant, Hayden & Whilden, of Charleston, S.C.; and Canfield Brothers of Baltimore, Md.

There were also a few men, like James Conning of Mobile, Ala., who apparently made a few presentation swords, or imported them "in the rough," ornamented them and marked them with their name.

At the outbreak of the war, several Southern States and the newly formed Confederate Government sent agents to the North to purchase weapons. Swords, and sabres, were included in these purchases, but few of them reached the South.

As many swords used in the Confederate Army were captured from the enemy, a glance at the types used in the Union Army is interesting.

General Ripley, Union Chief of Ordnance, reported June 30, 1862, that since the outbreak of the war, the Washington Government had purchased the following:

	American Made	European Made
Officers swords	1,352	2,107
Non-comm. officers	6,8899	19,951
Musicians swords	2,050	5,363
Cavalry sabres	53,986	138,813
Horse Artillery sabres	5,250	3,515
Foot Artillery swords	300	4,262

Col. George L. Schuyler, was sent to Europe by the Washington War Department and made extensive purchases of arms. In Sept. 1861, he wrote to the Secretary of War, that he had contracted for "20,000 light cavalry sabres of the Montmorency pattern."

Washington also let large contracts for sabres in the North. Perhaps the largest of these Northern swordmakers was the Ames Manufacturing Co., of Chicopee, Mass., an old firm of cutlers. They turned out excellent cavalry and artillery sabres of a pattern which remained unchanged and was the United States Army regulation until after the Spanish American War of 1898. Among other Northern sword makers was Tiffany, New York jeweler, who made fine weapons. The Confederate Government also sent agents to Europe in search of arms. General Josiah L. Gorgas, Confederate Chief of Ordnance, reported February 3, 1863, that Maj. Caleb Huse had bought abroad and shipped to the South by blockade runners, 16,178 cavalry sabres. There is no record, though, to show whence they came. The blockade runner *Fingal*, landed at Savannah in October, 1861, 500 cavalry sabres, and 250 swords of English make.

The United States Consul at Hamburg, Germany, reported April 5, 1862, that the British blockade runner *Bahama's* cargo included 57 boxes of cavalry swords marked "D.S." and 16 boxes marked "P.W."

That the business of running European arms through the blockade to the Confederacy continued until the last is shown by the announcement of the Navy Department in Washington on March 2, 1865, of the capture off the Florida coast of the British schooner *Delia* with a cargo of pig lead and sabres.

These English cavalry sabres were among the best

swords used in the South, and thousands of them were imported. They were called "Enfield sabres," and were adopted in 1853 for the British cavalry. Like the Enfield sabre bayonets, the grip was formed of two pieces of leather, or gutta percha riveted to the metal. Isaacs & Co., of London furnished many of these sabres to the South. To keep the record clear, however, it should be said that not all the Southern troopers liked these English sabres. Musgrove, in his book *Kentucky Cavaliers in Dixie*, says the 4th Kentucky Cavalry was issued these heavy English sabres which were unpopular (page 183).

Beautiful ornamented swords for officers were made in England and sent through the blockade by Robert Mole & Sons, of Birmingham; Firmin, of London, an old firm of military outfitters, and others.

Most of the swords bearing the name of Courtney & Tennant, Charleston, S.C., were made in England. The Charleston firm did not manufacture them.

Confederate swords were also made in Germany. W. Walsoneid, of Solingen, made many swords for the Confederacy.

The manufacture of swords was undertaken by many Southerners at the beginning of the war. *Debow's Review*, for March-April, 1862, says:

"McKennie & Co., of Charlottesville, Va., is making 6 swords a week.

"T.D. Driscoll, Howardsville, Va., is making 28 swords a week.

"W.J. McElroy & Co., of Macon, Ga., is making 20 infantry swords, 20 naval cutlasses, 20 sergeant's swords, and 20 bowie knives per week."

General Gideon Pillow, in a letter written from Memphis, Tenn., May 31, 1861, to General Anderson, says:

"We have a thousand sabres under way, none finished. In a few days we shall be receiving 50 a day."

These were probably made by Thomas Leech & Co., of the Memphis Novelty Works. As Memphis was taken by the enemy in June, 1862, the industry must have been short-lived, although after the fall of Memphis, Leech did continue his arms-making activities elsewhere.

In Richmond, swords and sabre bayonets were made by Boyle Gamble and MacFee. In the *Richmond Examiner* of September 2, 1861, there is a note that the firm's stock of steel had been badly damaged by fire the previous day. This factory was located at the foot of S. Seventh Street, near the Tredegar Iron Works.

There are frequent references in Southern newspapers of the war period to sword making, but in most instances it has been impossible to identify the products of these individuals and firms.

The *Richmond Examiner* for June 3, 1861, says that local armorers are making fine Bowie knives and could as easily make swords. "It is a mistake," says the editor, "to pay fancy prices for Ames chilled iron. Patronize home industries."

In the *Southern Confederacy*, published in Atlanta, Ga., June 22, 1864, is the advertisement of C.J. Christopher, "swordmaker, Bridge St., near the Bridge." Mr. Christopher offered to "repair swords of every description with neatness and dispatch."

The same newspaper also contained the advertisement of H. Marshall & Co., swordmakers. The swords of Christopher and Marshall, have remained unidentified.

The *Memphis Appeal* for November 3, 1861, says: "The *Savannah Republican* has been shown a sword made without machinery by Mr. B.P. Freeman, of Macon, which in solidarity, shape, and finish is not excelled in Yankeedom, or elsewhere. All honor to our energetic mechanics."

The *Richmond Examiner* for June 7, 1861, said a sword factory was being established at Tilton, Ga. The output of this factory, if it ever got into production, cannot be identified.

In the Acts of the Confederate Congress for May 9, 1861, there is a reference to "certain papers from R. W. Habersham, of South Carolina, touching on a new artillery sabre, and asking that it be tested."

An interesting note on sword making is contained in Wells, *Hampton and his Cavalry*. Says Wells: "At Columbia were made the heavy, long, straight, double edged swords, very serviceable and Crusader-like, with cross hilts."

This writer however is convinced that Wells is in error. He must have been confused as to the type of guard.

In the Confederate Museum in Richmond, are four regulation French dragoon sabres, with long straight, double edged blades, and four-branched guard. They are the type used by Napoleon's cavaliers at Waterloo.

Two of these French swords belonged to Gen. Wade Hampton, the third was given by Hampton to Gen. M.C. Butler, and the fourth was given by Hampton to Brig. Gen. Bradley T. Johnson of Maryland.

It must have been the above type swords to which Wells was referring. However, close examination will show that they are definitely of French manufacture.

A similar French dragoon sabre was carried by Col. Frederick Gustavus Skinner, of the 1st Virginia Regiment. It is dated 1814, and has a 38-inch blade. The sword was presented to the Colonel by Lafayette on the occasion of his visit to America in 1824.

At First Manassas, Col. Skinner is said to have slain three Federal cannonneers with this sword. At Second Manassas, Col. Skinner killed one enemy with this sword, and was then struck down by two bullets. The sword is still preserved by the Colonel's family (from *A Sporting Family of the Old South,* pp. 28, 42, and 44).

Kraft, Goldschmidt and Kraft, also operated a sword factory in Columbia, S.C. Some were made in South Carolina, while others were imported from England, and the blades etched by the South Carolina firm.

In some cases the Confederate swords made by this firm bear merely the initials "K. G. & K." Still others modeled after the regulation Ames sabres of the Union Army, are stamped simply "Columbia, S.C." Obviously they were made by Kraft, Goldschmidt and Kraft.

In the *Diary of General Gorgas*, the Confederate Chief of Ordnance, is this note of July 1st, 1864: "The President (Davis) sent for me day before yesterday to show me a big sword made at Columbia, S.C., and sent to him. He seemed to think highly of it tho I objected to its length." Under date of August 14, 1864, Gorgas writes: "He (Davis) spoke again of a long sabre that General Hampton wanted made for his cavalry, and remembered that on a previous occasion he spoke of armament of cavalry and said that if they had sabres they should not have guns, but be made to depend upon the sabre. He referred to the pistol carbine, the barrel of which was 12 inches long, and had a removable stock, which he had adopted in the United States service when Secretary of War. . . . He thought that if our cavalry were to depend upon the sabre alone that they would come to close quarters and run off their antagonists who depended upon their long range runs."

The largest sword factory in the South was the

Haiman plant at Columbus, Ga. Writing from Columbus under date of May 22, 1924, to the late E. Berkley Bowie of Baltimore, Md., one David Wolfson said in part:

"I was connected with the Haiman sword factory, and know all the particulars. They made swords, sabres, and army revolvers. We employed over 500 people, two of whom were from Virginia, and were experts in the manufacture of the Colt army pistol. The demands were so large that we had to annex a leather works to make boxes and straps to carry the cartridges, and also opened . . . a foundry to make cooking utensils for the army. The proprietors of the establishment were Louis, and Elias Haiman. Both are now dead (1924). Elias Haiman went to Europe and sent material through to us by the blockade. These works were carried on until the close of the war, when the Federals came in, as the last battle of the war was fought just across the river here at what is called Alabama Heights, and they destroyed the works at that time, on April 16, 1865."

That at times the Confederates had to go far afield for their swords is shown by the fact that in the Confederate Museum, Richmond, is a Persian yataghan, carried by a Confederate officer, and in the Springfield, Mass. Museum is a Turkish scimitar captured from a Confederate soldier.

The Confederate naval cutlasses were nothing about which to boast. Most of them were modeled after the type used in the U.S. Navy in the Mexican War, with short double-edged blades similar to those of the obsolete foot artillery sword.

Some of these cutlasses were exactly like the foot artillery swords, and lacked the hand guards. They had merely the short straight cross-hilt. With the clumsy blades several inches shorter than those of the Ames cutlass used in the Union Navy, the Confederate sailor was at a great disadvantage when facing his better-armed adversary.

The British bayonet cutlass, run through the blockade from England, was a much better weapon than those manufactured in the South. But England also sent to the Confederacy the short double-edged blade cutlass as well.

One in the Battle Abbey collection has a brass guard like that of the enfield sabre, and with the same gutta-percha, or leather grip. The 20-inch blade is encased in a black leather scabbard with brass tip and mouthpiece. On the back of the blade near the hilt is stamped "Mole," showing that it was made by Robert Mole of Birmingham, England. On the side of the blade is stamped "Courtney & Tennant, Charleston, S. C.," the firm which imported the weapon. These cutlasses are also found with a solid brass guard instead of the three-branched one described above.

The experts seem to differ about the efficiency of these short double-edged cutlasses. Commander Palmer, of the U.S.S. *Iroquois*, on September 4, 1861, complained that his Sharps rifles had no sword bayonets and that his cutlasses were all worthless old-fashioned Roman swords (*Official Records,* Vol. VI, p. 168).

On the other hand, Col. John Taylor Wood, of the Confederate Army, in a report of his dashing exploit in the Rappahannock River, wrote:

"In August, 1863, I left Richmond with four boats, and 60 men, and off Cawtoman's boarded the U.S.S. *Satellite,* and *Reliance.* We dashed alongside, and cut our way through the boarding nettings with the old Navy cutlass, or Roman sword, by far the most effective weapon for this work" (*Jeff. Davis Constitutionalist*, Vol. VIII, p. 543).

An article in the Louisville, Ky., *Journal* of March 9, 1865, says: "The Confederates captured at Chapman's Landing each had a fine Enfield rifle musket, and a regular Navy cutlass. One of the cutlasses was shown us. Including the handle it is two feet six inches long, and the blade is nearly two inches wide. On the handle are the letters 'C.S.N.'"

Undoubtedly these men carried the British Enfield cutlass bayonet, such as was used on some of the Enfield rifles, and the Wilson breech loading rifle which was used in the Confederate Navy.

No account of Confederate swords would be complete without some mention of the Virginia Manufactory sabres, which have been a subject of much controversy. Captain Theodore T. Belote in his excellent catalogue of swords in the National Museum, Washington, published in 1932, calls them "Hessian sabres." But in the Bulletin of the American Sword Collectors Society for October 1947, he says that he is not prepared to argue that designation.

The writer believes they were made at the Virginia Manufactory, or Richmond Armory, but can submit no documentary proof of this theory. The Virginia Manufactory, or State Armory, was authorized by the Virginia Legislature of 1798, and began operations in March, 1802. By October, 1803, John Clarke, Superintendent of the Armory reported that they had made and had in storage 3,272 muskets, 14 rifles, 470 pistols, 405 cavalry sabres, and 50 artillery swords.

Another document gives the output for 1806,

which included 852 cavalry swords, 444 iron scabbards, and 164 artillery swords.

On April 17, 1861, the day Virginia seceded, Adjutant General William Harvey Richardson reported to Governor Letcher that 3,350 cavalry sabres were in the hands of Virginia horse militia.

In 1863, General Charles Dimmick, Virginia Chief of Ordnance, reported to the Legislature that the Richmond Armory had issued up to October 1, 1863, 7,863 sabres, of which the majority were "Virginia sabres."

An article in the *Columbian, South Carolinian* for January 3, 1861, telling of Virginia's preparation for defense, says that old muskets, and rifles made at the Richmond Armory were being altered from flintlock to percussion and adds: "A quantity of old sabres owned by the State, 500 in Richmond, and 1,000 in Lexington, have been shortened and scabbarded and are now of modern design."

The fact is that the Virginia troopers complained of the weight and length of the old sabres. As a result, hundreds of them were made over by having the blades shortened by five inches, made narrower near the point, and fitted with new scabbards of iron with brass rings, and mouthpiece.

In the Virginia archives of the war years in the State Library at Richmond, are frequent references to "Old Virginia Sabres," "Virginia Cavalry sabres," and "Virginia sabres with new scabbards." On January 21, 1861, the Virginia Ordnance Department recorded the receipt of 2,000 new cavalry sabres, and 468 Virginia cavalry sabres with new scabbards (document-State Library).

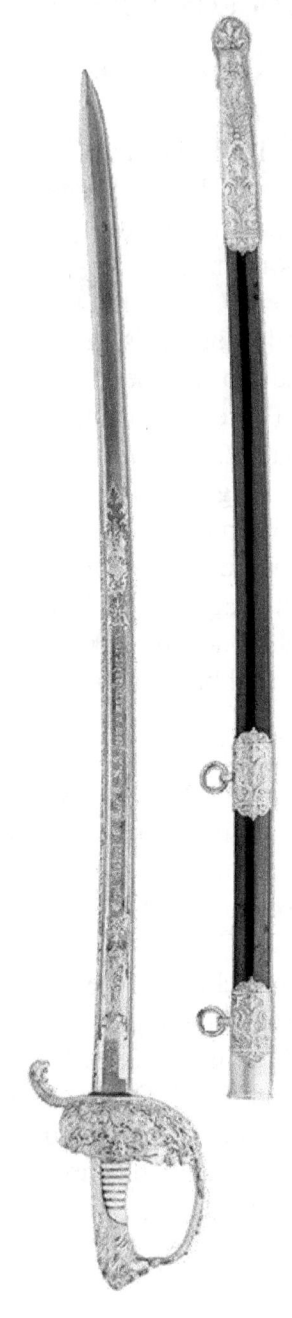

Plate 1: The ceremonial sword of Gen. Robert E. Lee, now displayed in the Museum of the Confederacy, Richmond, Va.

ONE
The Sword of General Robert E. Lee, C.S.A.

The most cherished sword of the South is that one which belonged to Gen. Robert E. Lee. It is this sword that he wore at Appomattox, and many present at that famous conference commented upon its beauty. This priceless relic is in the Virginia Room at the Confederate Museum, Richmond. It was given to the General by an unknown Marylander in 1863, and aside from its historical value which has no limits, it is of itself of high intrinsic worth, and a fine example of the sword maker's art. The blade is almost straight, 34 inches long, 1 1/8 inches wide, beautifully etched with floral designs and trophies. The obverse bears the inscription "Gen'l Robert E. Lee, C.S.A., from a marylander, 1863." (note that Marylander is spelled with a small "m"). The reverse bears the French inscription "Aide toi et Dieu L'aidera." The grip is of ivory wound with 10 turns of 3 stranded gilt wire. The pommel and back-strap form a lion's head. The guard is exquisitely made showing floral designs and a shield bearing a cross. The counterguard contains in relief floral designs, draped figures, and a snake twined about the branches. The maker's name "Devisme a Paris" appears on the back of the blade. Over-all length 40 inches. The scabbard is of polished gunmetal with ornamented brass mounts.

All efforts to definitely establish the donor of this gift have been unsuccessful.

Dr. Douglas S. Freeman, author of the 4-volume *Life of Lee*, says he has no idea of the identity of the "Marylander."

Mr. Richard D. Steuart, co-author of this present work, modestly suggests that it was Samuel H. Tagart of Baltimore, Md., intimate friend of Lee. Lee stayed at the Tagart home in Baltimore both before and after the war. It is inconsistent with Lee's character that he would accept so valuable a gift from anyone save an intimate friend.

Another sword by Devisme, was carried by General John B. Hood, C.S.A., and is in the Texas Room of the same museum. This sword is of the 3-branch variety, very similar to the one carried by Gen. J.E.B. Stuart, also in this same museum. In appearance, almost identical with a sword made by Thomas Griswold & Co., and pictured in Plate No. 7.

TWO
James Conning
Mobile, Alabama
☆ ☆ ☆ ☆

James Conning has been something of an enigma to historians, because he must have made swords for a long time, and was better known as a silversmith. Stephen Ensko, in his *American Silversmiths*, lists him as a New York silversmith of about 1840. However, at about that time he must have removed to Mobile, Ala., as swords have been found bearing his name, and obviously of that period.

One sword, with ivory grip and eagle's head pommel, and of the period 1816-1840, bears on the brass mouthpiece of the leather scabbard: "Made by James Conning Mobile Ala. 1776." The serial No. 20 is stamped in the blade. The date of 1776, if it is a date, is unexplainable. On the other side of the mouthpiece in script is the name "J.H. Carr."

Conning made many swords for the Confederacy. In the Battle Abbey collection, Richmond, Va., is a regulation artillery sabre, with 28-inch curved blade, wooden, wire-wound grip, single brass knuckle guard, and iron scabbard. Stamped on the blade is "James Conning, Ala.," and on the brass guard is "State of Ala., 1862" and

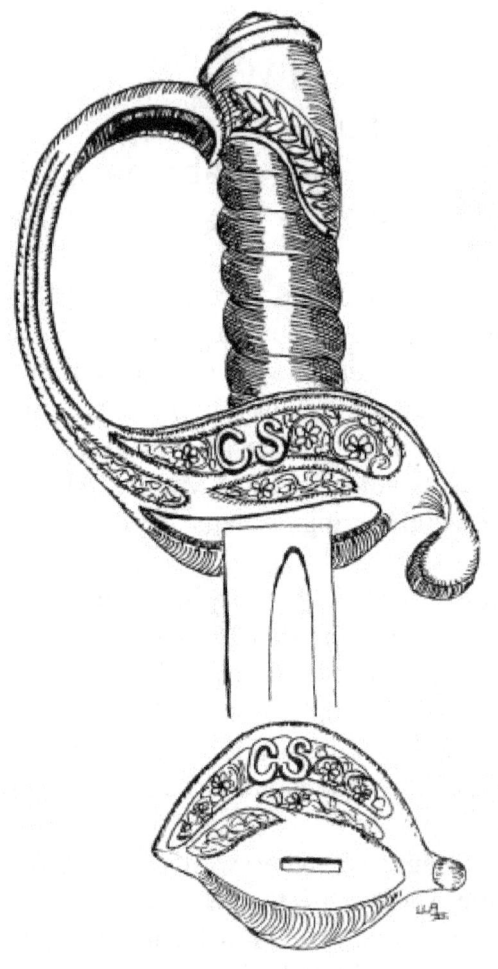

Plate 2

the serial No. 127.

The most familiar sword made by Conning is the one which conforms with the deep-hilted field officer's sword of the Civil War period, and is a creditable imitation of its U.S. counterpart. The guard bears the letters "CS" in large capitals, but not so well cast as the U.S. weapon.

One U.S. sword of this type was carried by Gen. "Stonewall" Jackson until his death, and may now be seen in the Confederate Museum in Richmond, Va.

A C.S. sword by Conning is shown on the accompanying page. This weapon gives no clue as to the identity of the maker, and bears no marks except the serial stamped on blade, and scabbard band. The guard is of brass, well cast, with "C.S." in large letters between the branches. The pommel is decorated with a leaf design. Two swords of this type are in the Battle Abbey, one with a blade etched with floral design and the letters "C.S." in old English.

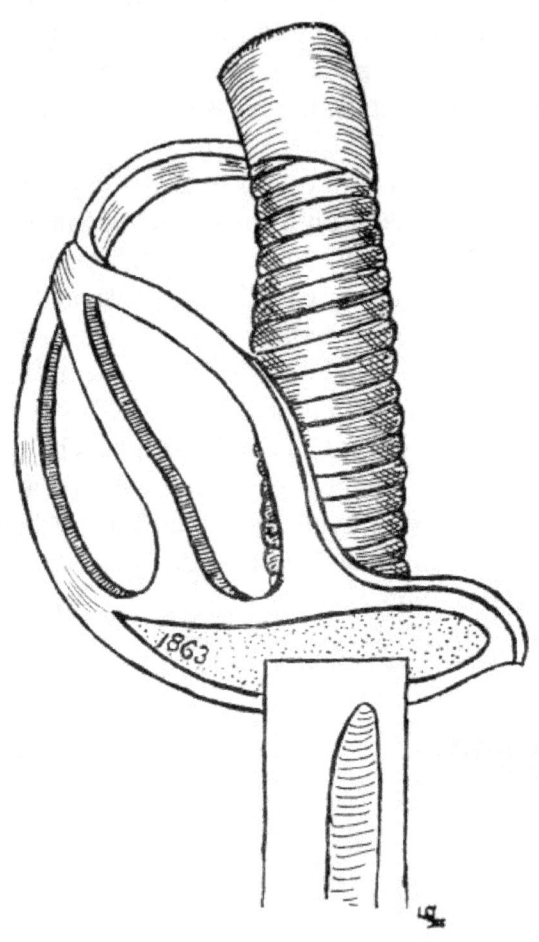

Plate 3

THREE
Tallassee, Alabama

Imitations of the U.S. Cavalry sabre were made for the Confederacy at Tallassee, Ala., and the pictured sabre is believed to have been made there.

This sabre closely imitates the U.S. Cavalry model, but the guard appears to have been stamped out of sheet brass, although actually it was cast. The branches are flat rather than round. The 35-inch blade is curved, 1 1/8 inches wide, with single shallow groove on either side for a blood gutter. The grip is wrapped with oilcloth, and wound with iron wire. The pommel is distinctive, being conical in shape and undecorated. The scabbard is of metal with brass mounts, and brass rings.

The letters "C.S.A." have been stamped on the back of the guard, and the date "1863" is stamped on the underside. As far as is known these stampings are genuine, although many have been seen which carried no markings of any kind.

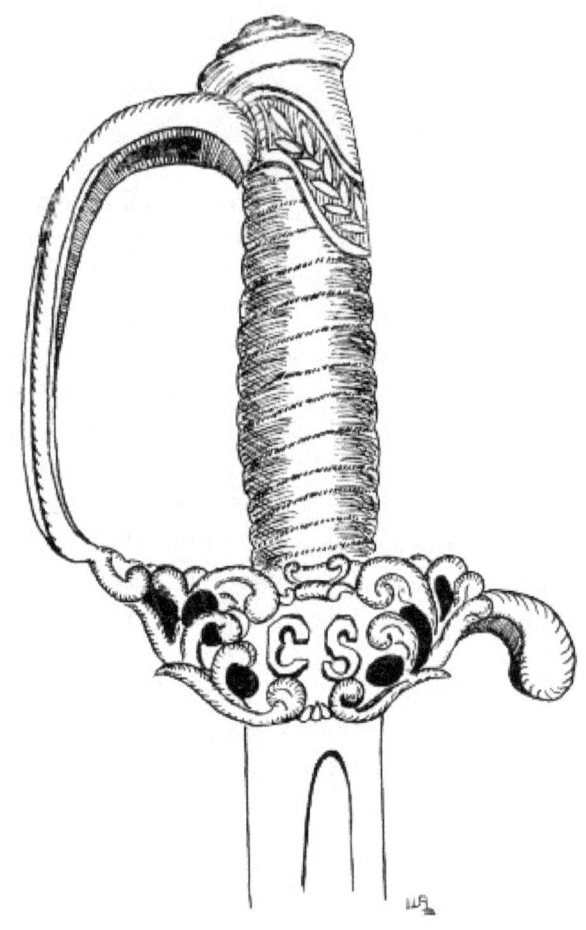

Plate 4

FOUR
L. Haiman & Brother
Columbus, Ga.

The weapon on the opposite page was made by L. Haiman & Bro., Columbus, Ga., and is so marked on the blade. Blade is also etched with floral designs, trophies, and "C.S.A." The grip is of black leather wound with double-stranded brass wire. Guard is well cast with a counterguard that turns down. It bears in raised letters "C.S." The scabbard is iron with brass mountings. A similar sword is in the Confederate Museum, Richmond, and belonged to Capt. E. V. White, C.S.N., engineer on the ironclad *Virginia*. The blade of this sword is nicely etched, with the letters "C.S.," but no maker's name.

In the Battle Abbey collection is still a third sword of this type, with "Deo Vindice" etched on the blade and the name "L. Haiman & Bro., Columbus, Ga."

Also in the Battle Abbey are two other presentation swords made by the Haimans. One is an officer's sword, with 32-inch blade and brass mounted black leather scabbard. On one side of the blade is etched a scroll, cannon, tents, and "C.S.," and the name "E. G. Dawson" in Old English letters. On the other side of the blade are flags, and "Terrell Artillery." On the back of the blade is etched "C.S. Spear," and stamped "L. Haiman & Bro."

The other sword is also of officer type with brass open guard, leather, wire-wound grip, leather scabbard and 33-inch curved blade. On one side of the blade is etched a stand of colors, and "C.S.A." On the other side is "Capt. E.G. Dawson, presented by L. Haiman & Bro." Both of these swords belonged to Capt. Edgar G. Dawson, commanding the Terrell Light Artillery of Georgia.

FIVE
L. Haiman & Brother
(continued)

One of the most successful munitions plants in the Confederacy was that of Louis Haiman & Bro., at Columbus, Ga.

Louis, and Elias Haiman, were natives of Prussia, but came to this country when very young. They settled in Columbus, then a small village, and grew up with the place. At the outbreak of the war, they were engaged in making kitchen utensils. They first opened a sword factory, later a rifle factory, and still later a plant for the manufacture of Colt-model revolvers. The last named was the Columbus Fire Arms Manufacturing Co.

The sword factory employed several hundred hands and turned out 100 swords a week. The first sword made was presented to Col. Peyton H. Colquitt, later killed at Chicamauga. It was a beautiful weapon, inlaid with gold.

Another Haiman sword of great beauty is in the Confederate Museum, Richmond. It belonged to Gen. Henry D. Clayton, of Alabama. The blade is straight, 34 inches long, and richly etched. It bears the following inscription: "Chicamauga, Sept. 19, 20, 1863; Murfreesboro, Dec. 30th, & 31st, 1862; Pensacola, Nov. 22nd, &

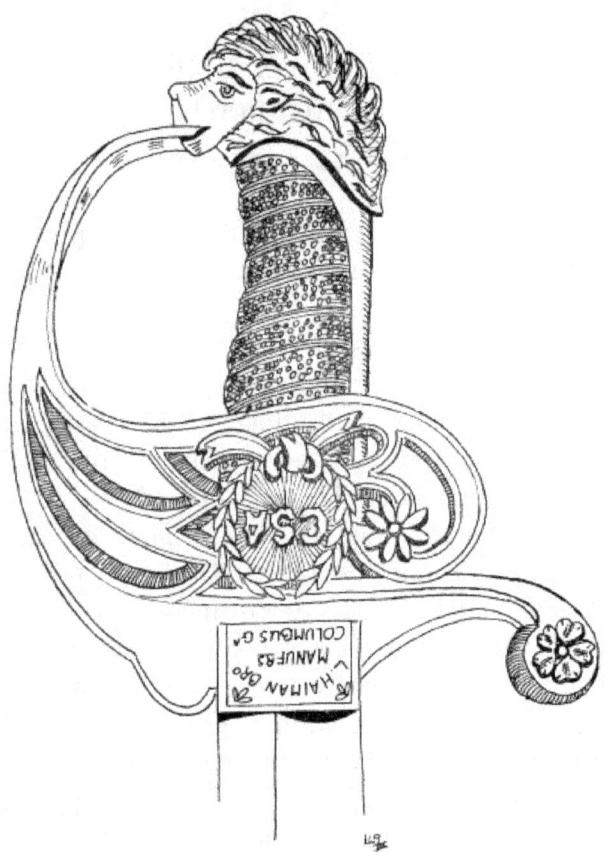

Plate 5

23rd, 1861; Deo Vindice; Virtus Nobilitat." On the reverse near the hilt is etched; "L. Haiman & Bro. manufs., Columbus, Ga." On the back of the blade is etched "Ironproof." The guard is of brass, gold-plated, and of intricate design. In the counterguard are three large letters: "C.S.A." The pommel is a lion's head. The grip is of sharkskin wound with seven turns of three-stranded gilt wire. The scabbard is of iron with brass mounts. The guard and grip of this sword are so typically English as to suggest importation.

A sword of similar design, also in the Confederate Museum, was presented to Gen. Archibald Gracie. His initials, "A.G." instead of the C.S.A. appear in the counterguard. The grip is of leather instead of sharkskin. On the blade is etched "C.S.A., Gen. Archibald Gracie, presented by Lieut. E.B. Cherry" Midway of the blade in an oval is etched "L. Haiman & Bro."

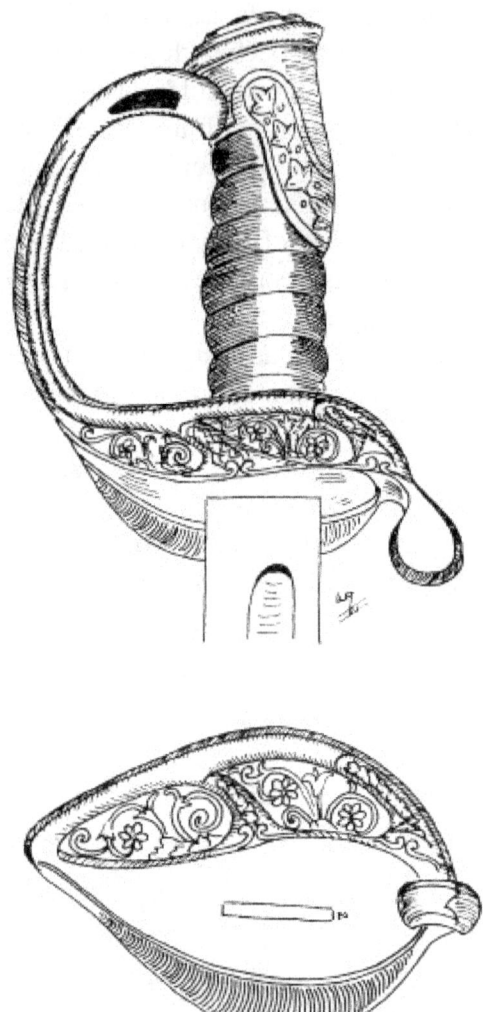

Plate 6

SIX
Macon, Georgia
E.J. Johnston & Co.
W.J. McElroy

This pictured sword has a straight 30-inch blade, 1 inch wide, is lightly etched with vines, trophies, a furled Confederate flag, and on the reverse, midway of the blade, the large capital letters, "C.S.A." A tapering shallow blood gutter is on either side. The grip is of leather wound with ten turns of single strand brass wire. The guard conforms to the U.S. Foot officer's swords of this period, but is rough and unfinished in appearance. The number 2 is stamped on the underside of the guard. The pommel is decorated with ivy leaves. The scabbard is of leather with three brass mounts. I have had at least six or more of these swords, most of them similarly etched, and most being stamped on the guard and pommel with a number. I have never known the maker.

A foot officer's sword similar in general appearance is in the National Museum in Washington, D.C., and is described as follows: 30-inch blade, 1 inch wide, with slightly rounded back, almost straight, with tapering blood gutter on either side. It is etched with floral designs with large "C.S." on one side, and "E.J. Johnston & Co.,

Macon, Ga." on the other. The guard is of cast brass, with standard rose design in the counterguard. The grip is of leather wound with thirteen turns of single stranded brass wire. The pommel is decorated with a leaf design. The scabbard is of leather with brass mounts.

W. J. McElroy, another sword manufacturer for the Confederacy, also operated in Macon, Ga. According to *DeBow's Review* of March-April 1862, he was turning out twenty infantry swords, twenty naval cutlasses, twenty sergeant's swords, and twenty Bowie knives per week, and so his contribution to the Confederacy in his line must have been considerable, although specimens bearing his name are rare. There are, however, two in the Battle Abbey collection, both with etched blades and "W. J. McElroy & Co., Macon, Ga." Scabbards were of leather, brass mounted.

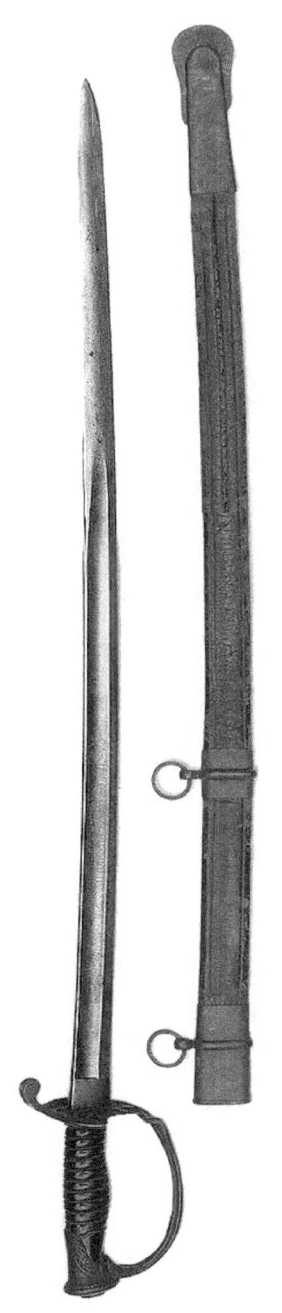

E. J. Johnston & Co. Confederate Foot Officer Sword

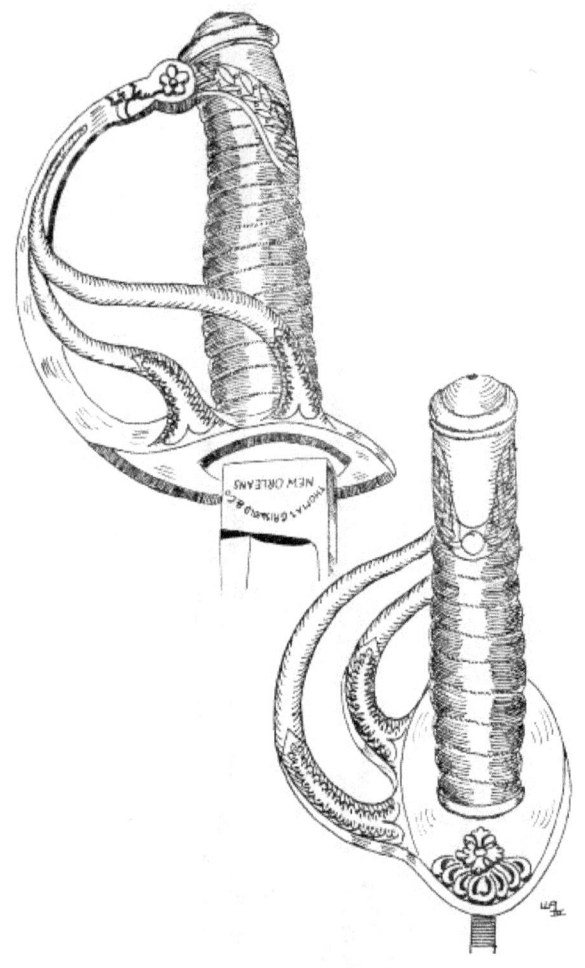

Plate 7

SEVEN
Thomas, Griswold & Co.
New Orleans, La.

The firm of Thomas, Griswold & Co., was an outgrowth of the old importing company of Hyde & Goodrich, which operated in New Orleans until the summer of 1861. A.B. Griswold, was apparently the head of the new firm, which operated until the fall of New Orleans, and turned out a large variety of swords, cutlasses, and sabres.

The cavalry sabre pictured has a very curved blade, 34 inches long, 1 1/8 inches wide with a flat back, and a wide shallow blood gutter on either side. Stamped on the reverse near the hilt (shown in the picture on the obverse) is the maker's name, "Thomas Griswold & Co., New Orleans." The grip is of brown leather wound with double stranded brass wire. The guard is copied from the popular French Cavalry officer's sabre of this period, with decorated branches and guard. The pommel is decorated with leaf design. The scabbard is made entirely of brass. The weapon has a decidedly finished appearance, and compares favorably with those turned out by the Federal Government. Over-all length 39 inches.

A sword of this type is in the Battle Abbey collection.

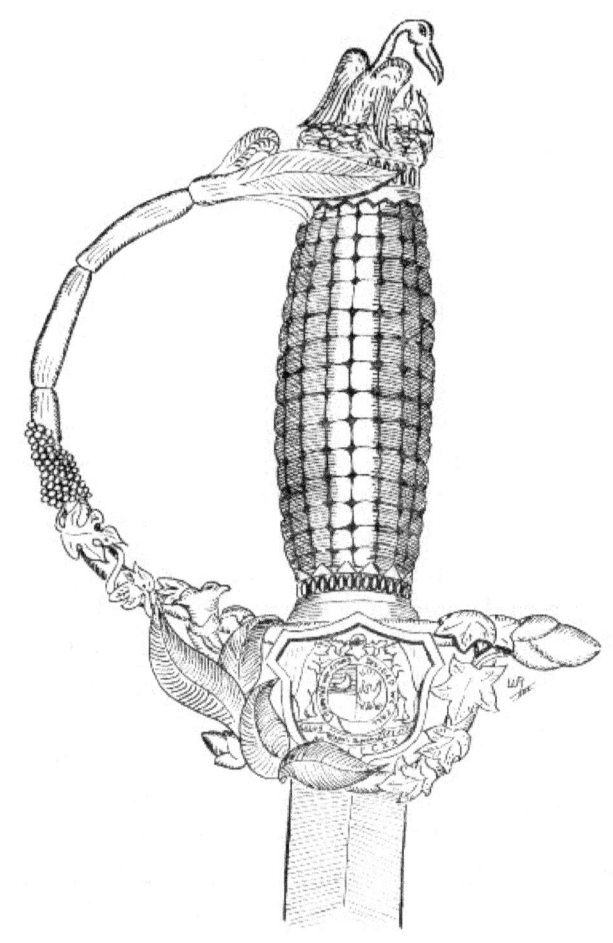

Plate 8

EIGHT
Thomas, Griswold & Co.
New Orleans, La.
(continued)

In the Confederate Museum in Richmond, Va., is a beautiful sword made by this firm, and which was presented to Gen. Sterling Price, C.S.A., by the women of New Orleans, in 1862, after the Battle of Lexington. The sword is designed to represent the States of Louisiana, and Missouri. The scabbard is of gold with ornamented ring mounts to represent the corn of Missouri, and the sugar cane of Louisiana. The grip is of ivory formed in the shape of an ear of corn. The counterguard contains the leaves of the hemp stalk, and tobacco for Missouri, and the cotton boll for Louisiana. A gold shield in the counterguard is engraved with the coat of arms of Missouri, while the pommel in gold in the shape of a pelican on her nest, is the arms of the State of Louisiana. The sword cost $1,000.00 which was raised by public subscription, and the largest amount anyone could give was $1.00, so that a large number could participate in the gift. The sword is enclosed in a wooden box, which is lined with gold plush.

The blade is 31 3/4 inches long, 1 inch wide, double-edged elaborately etched, the reverse containing cotton and tobacco plants, crossed cannon, and the letters "CS" in old English letters. The name "Thomas Griswold & Co., New Orleans" is stamped near the hilt. The obverse of the blade bears the inscription: "Ense et Virtute ner aspera ad alta."

A private collector now has a presentation piece made by Thomas, Griswold & Co., whose guard was formed by two twisted snakes. The grip was of ivory, and the pommel and backstrap in the shape of an eagle's head. The blade was finely etched, with the inscription showing that it had been presented to some colonel by the people of New Orleans. The maker's name was stamped on the throat of the blade. The scabbard was of leather with brass ring mounts.

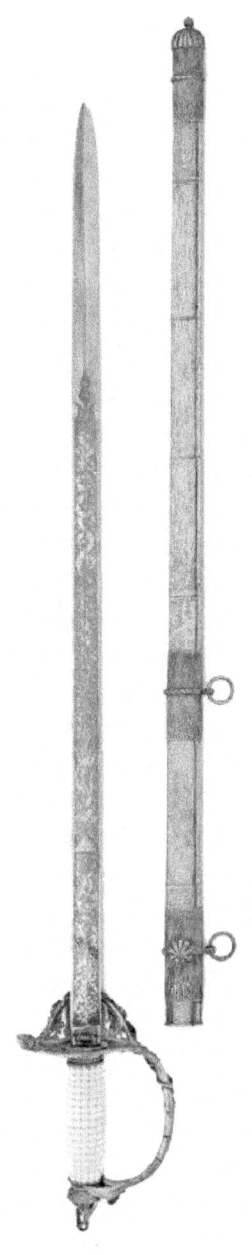

Decorative sword presented in 1862 to Gen. Sterling Price by the ladies of New Orleans.

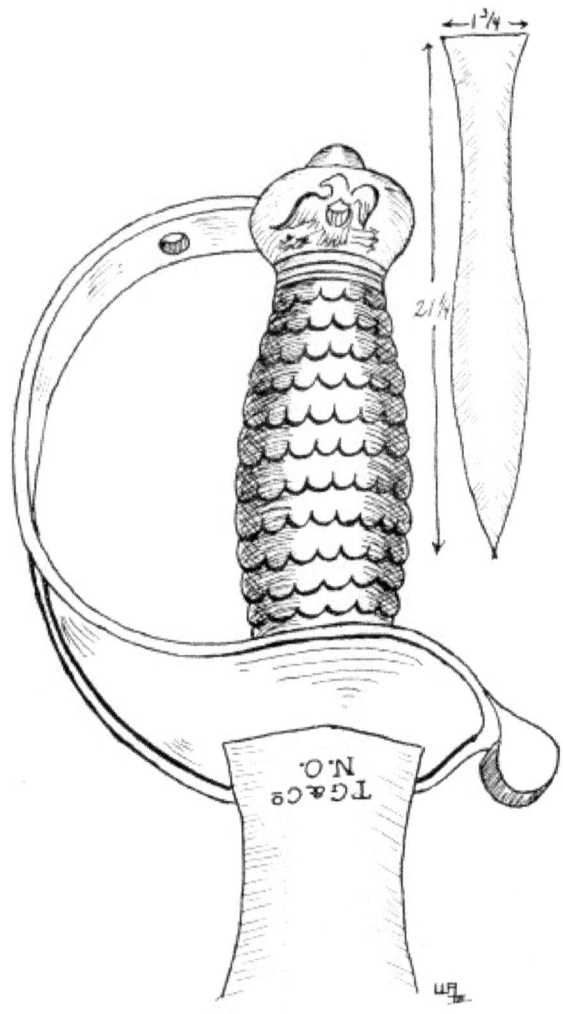

Plate 9

NINE
Thomas, Griswold & Co.
New Orleans, La.
(continued)

This is another sword by Thomas, Griswold and Co., of New Orleans, being a navy cutlass patterned after the U.S. Naval cutlasses of the Mexican War period.

The grip and guard are of heavy cast brass, the former being in imitation of fish scales. Cast into the obverse of the pommel is a spread eagle with shield and arrows. The blade is double-edged 21 1/4 inches long, 1 3/4 inches wide, with diamond cross section. The sword has an over-all length of 27 inches. The scabbard is of leather with two brass mounts.

Stamped in the blade near the hilt on the reverse (shown on obverse in the picture) are the letters: "T.G. & Co., N.O.," which of course stand for Thomas, Griswold & Co., New Orleans.

Another New Orleans arms manufacturer who also made swords was Cook & Co., which firm was operated by F.W.C. Cook.

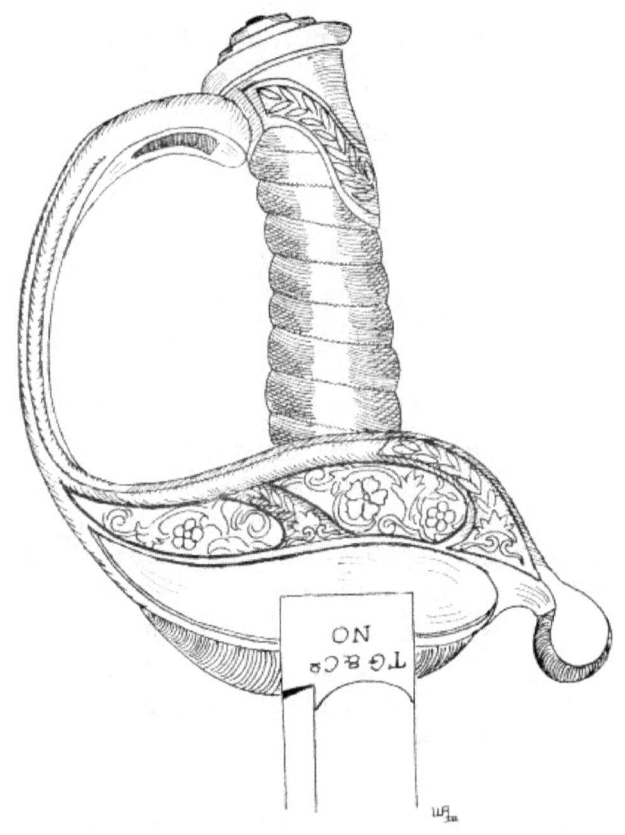

Plate 10

TEN
Thomas, Griswold & Co.
(continued)

A sword whose guard conforms to the regulation foot officer's pattern, and which was carried by Gen. Richard Taylor, C.S.A., is in the Confederate Museum in Richmond. This sword is in the Louisiana Room.

The blade is almost straight, 29 1/2 inches long, 1 inch wide, highly polished and undecorated. A shallow blood gutter is on either side, and stamped near the hilt on the reverse (shown on the obverse in the picture) are the letters, "T. G. & Co., N.O." standing for Thomas, Griswold & Co., New Orleans. The guard is of the regulation pattern, nicely cast in brass. The grip is covered with brown leather, wound with fourteen turns of double stranded brass wire. The pommel is decorated with a leaf design. The scabbard is of copper-brass with two brass ring mounts. Over-all length is 35 inches.

Another Griswold sword of this same type, which is now in the same museum, was carried by Gen. W.M. L. Jackson, C.S.A. of Virginia. The only difference in it and the one shown is that the Jackson sword has a leather scabbard with three brass mounts. The top mount is engraved: "Col. W.M.L. Jackson, from the 31st Reg., Va., Vol., 1861."

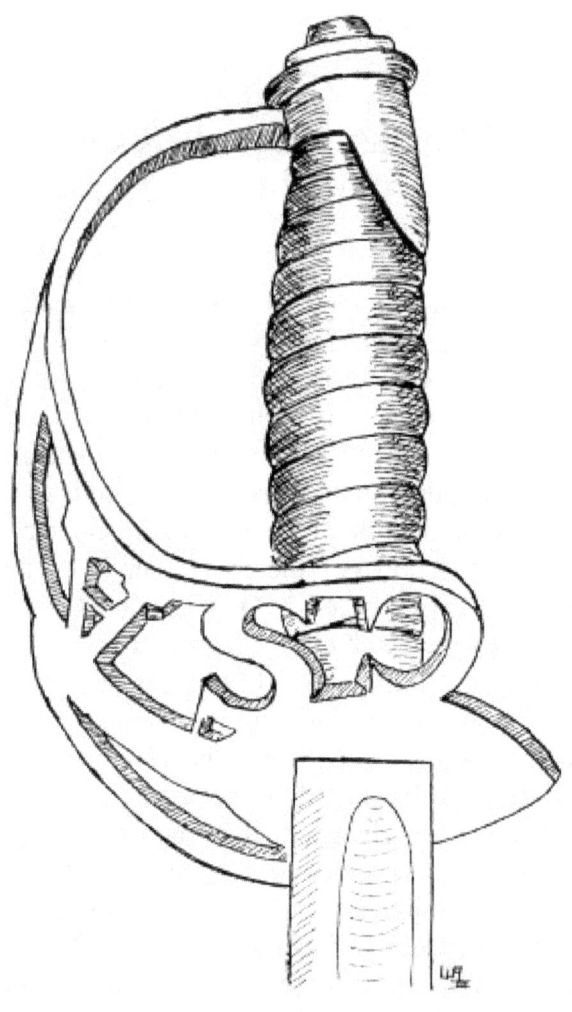

Plate 11

ELEVEN
Fayetteville, N.C.
☆ ☆ ☆ ☆

Among the Confederate swords that have survived the years, few are more interesting or are found more frequently than this one. While collectors agree that this sword was made in North Carolina, there is a great deal of disagreement as to who made them and where. One thought is that they were made by Louis Froelich at Kenansville, N.C., and another theory is that they were made in Fayetteville. Still another theory is that they were made at New Berne, N.C.

Of perhaps a dozen of these swords which have come to hand during a long period of collecting, practically all were found to bear a Roman numeral, cut into the side of the guard. This was probably a maker's mark, rather than a serial. The lowest number noted was VII; the highest was XXXVII.

Several swords of this type are in the National Museum in Washington, D.C., and are described in Bulletin No. 163, page 66.

The one pictured, now in the Battle Abbey, has a 32-inch straight blade, almost an inch in width, with a tapering blood gutter on each side. The guard appears to have been stamped out of sheet brass, but close examination reveals that it was actually cast. The guard and counterguard form the letters "C.S.A." The grip is of leather wound with thirteen turns of single strand iron wire, although some were wound with brass or copper wire. The scabbard is of metal and brass throat, toe, and ring mounts. The rings are of metal. Over-all length 37 1/4 inches.

A similar sword in a private collection is described as being stamped 1862, the letters "OSV," and what appears to be "Prov Tool Company."

Of the many examined this is the only one bearing any markings besides the Roman numeral. That so many have survived, despite their crude workmanship, indicates that a great number must have been made.

They are found only in the wake of the Army of Northern Virginia.

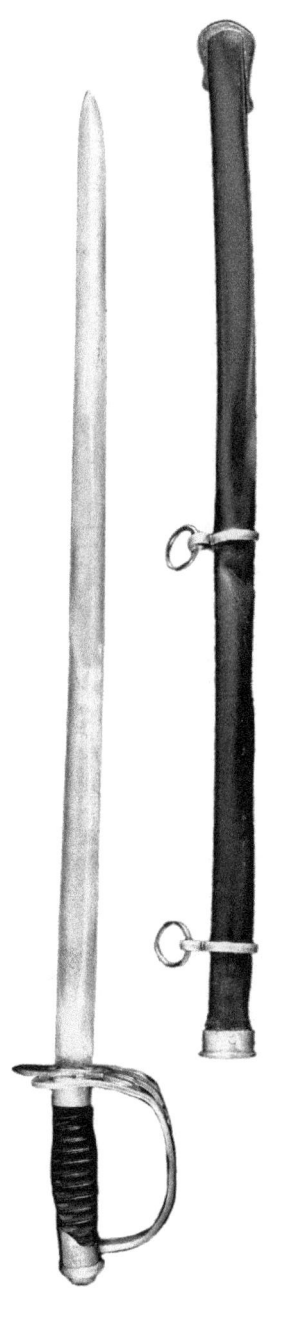

Sword thought to have been made in either Kenansville or Fayetteville, N.C.

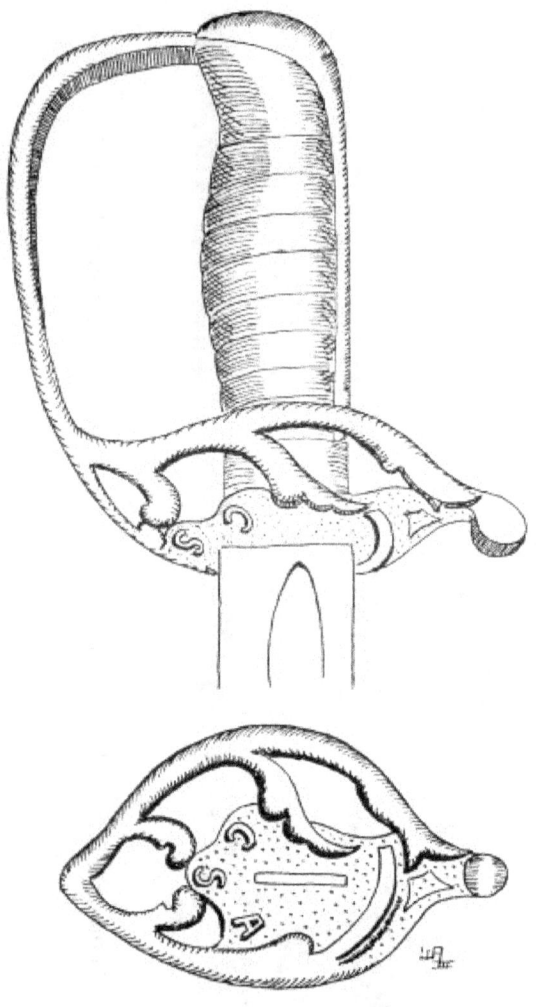

Plate 12

TWELVE
Louis Froelich
Kenansville, N.C.

A sword which is very similar to those put out by the Nashville Plow Works, and shown in Plate 17 of this book, is the one pictured in Plate 12. Comparison with that one done by the Nashville Plow Works, shows the casting to be identical, and apparently from the same pattern. The only difference is that the back strap is of metal, not brass, and the name "Nashville Plow Works" has been deleted from the guard. Both are cavalry sabres, same type of curved blade, and the scabbards are the same.

This sabre came to me with a damaged grip, and in repairing it the blade was unseated. On the tang of the blade, were the initials "L.B.F." stamped inside a rectangle, and which were evidently the maker's name, although it is possible that they were the individual worker's mark. The only known sword maker in the South whose initials could be L.B.F., would be Louis Froelich, who with Col. Eastvan, originally operated at Wilmington, N.C., and contracted to sell swords to the State of North Carolina. Shortly after the start of the war, Eastvan left the partnership, and later Froelich opened a factory employing some fifteen to twenty hands at Kenansville. This factory operated until destroyed by Gen. J.G. Foster, U.S.A., July, 1863.

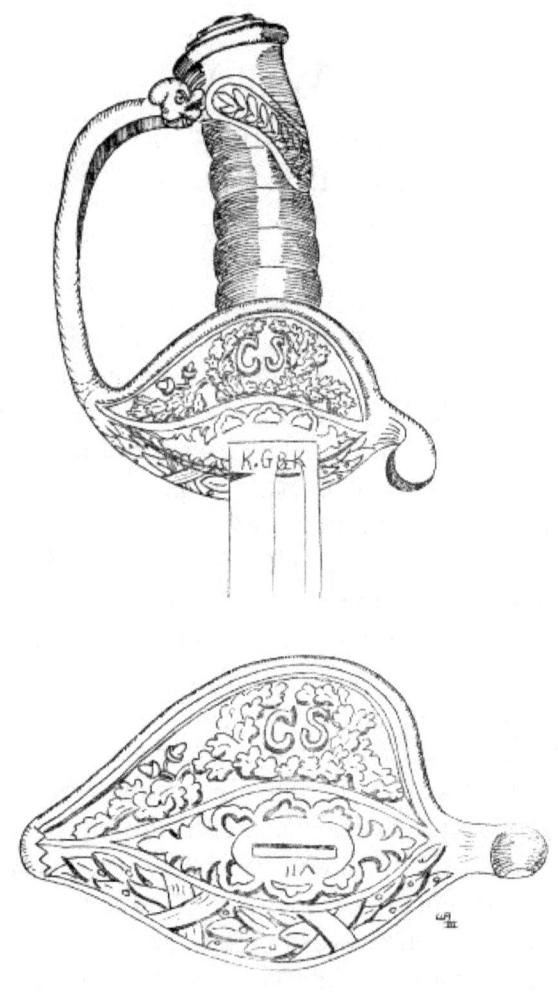

Plate 13

THIRTEEN
Kraft, Goldschmidt & Kraft
Columbia, S.C.

This firm made and imported many beautiful swords for the Confederacy, many of which bear the firm's full name, and others merely the initials, "K.G. & K." Peter W. was the head of the firm.

In the Battle Abbey collection in Richmond is a beautiful cavalry sabre which was used by Gen. William L. Jackson, cousin of "Stonewall," commanding Jenkins brigade of cavalry. The sword used by Gen. Jackson as an infantry colonel is in the Confederate Museum, Richmond.

The cavalry sabre has a slightly curved blade 35 3/4 inches long, double-edged near the end. It is finely etched with "C.S." in a wreath, and "Columbia, S.C." on one side. The other side has decorations and "Kraft, Goldschmidt & Kraft." There is a broad, heavy brass guard ornamented with an eagle, stand of colors, and wreath. The grip is of leather wound with wire, and there is a leather loop for the forefinger to insure a firmer grip. The pommel is a lion's head of brass. Scabbard is of iron and brass mouthpiece and tip, and two brass bands ornamented with the head of a helmeted warrior. It is probable that the sword was made in England, and the blade decorated in Columbia.

The one pictured is an officer's sword with straight blade 32 inches long, 1 1/4 inches wide, with a wide shallow blood gutter on either side. It is nicely etched with vines, tobacco plants, grapes, and the large letters "C.S." Near the hilt on the obverse is etched "K. G. & K." and on the reverse side, "Columbia, S.C." The hilt is wrapped with black leather wound with eight turns of single strand copper wire. The knuckle guard in joining the pommel is formed in the shape of a monster. The guard is of cast brass gold plated, decorated with leaves, and in the counterguard the large letters, "C.S." cast in a wreath of oak leaves. The scabbard is of metal with brass throat, toe and ring mounts. Several swords of this type are to be found in the Battle Abbey collection in Richmond.

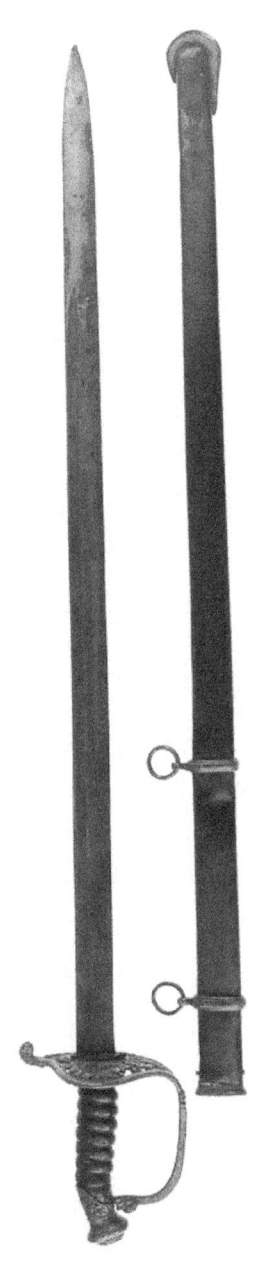

Sword made by Kraft, Goldschmidt & Kraft of Columbia, S.C.

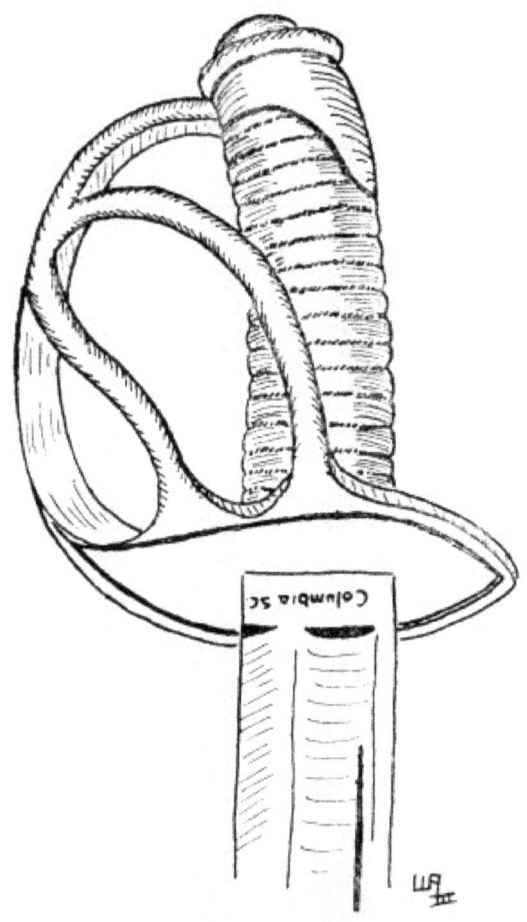

Plate 14

FOURTEEN
Kraft, Goldschmidt & Kraft (continued)

Another Columbia, S.C. sabre is the one pictured. This is a fine imitation of the U.S. Regulation 1840-50 cavalry model, with stopped blood gutter, and long curved blade. Grip is covered with leather, and wound with double stranded brass wire. Pommel is unornamented. Stamped on the reverse of the blade near the hilt (shown on the obverse in the picture) is "Columbia, S.C." The scabbard also conforms to the U.S. model, is of metal with metal ring mounts.

    The frequency with which these sabres turn up would indicate that quite a few were made. They are the finest Confederate made imitations of the U.S. model. A point that might be of interest to collectors is that the wooden grip was made without notches. It was then wrapped with light rope, covered with leather, then wound with the wire, the wire following the lines made by the rope, and giving the appearance that the grip itself was grooved.

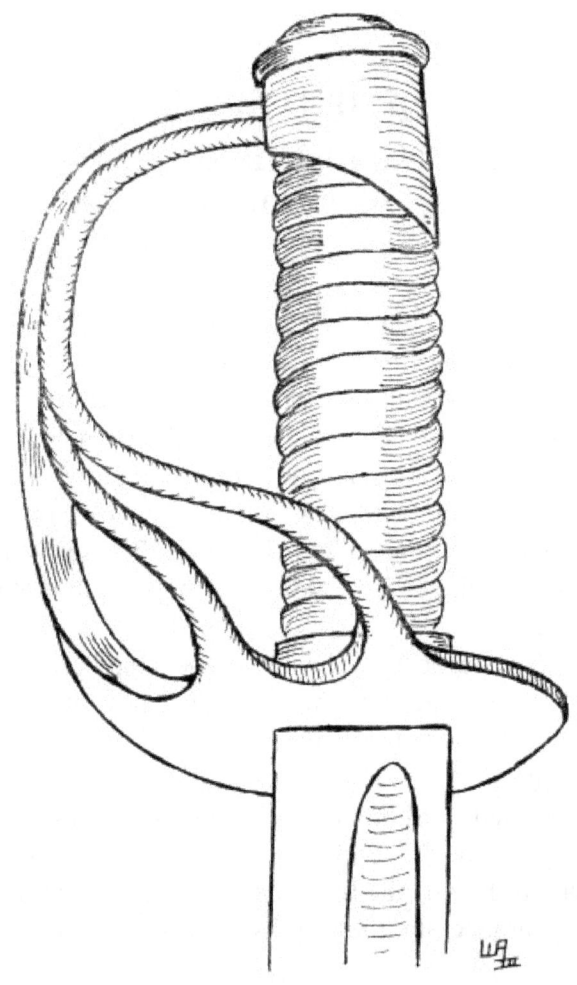

Plate 15

FIFTEEN
Columbia, S.C.
☆ ☆ ☆ ☆

This crude appearing weapon is reported to have been made in Columbia, S.C., but despite having examined a number of them, none were found to be marked in any way.

One of these cavalry sabres now in the Battle Abbey collection was found near the Kelly House on the Battlefield of Chicamauga. It has a 35-inch straight blade, 1 1/4 inches wide. Over-all length is 40 3/4 inches. The guard is cast brass, but gives the general appearance of having been stamped from a flat piece rather than cast. Grip is covered with leather wound with thirteen turns of single stranded iron wire. Pommel is undecorated.

All swords of this type examined were found to have cedar wood scabbards with metal throat, toe, and ring mounts. Some were made with brass ring mounts, but most apparently of iron.

Sabres with wooden scabbards were issued to the Fifth Georgia Cavalry of Wheeler's command in the early part of 1865 (*Confederate Veteran*, August 1924).

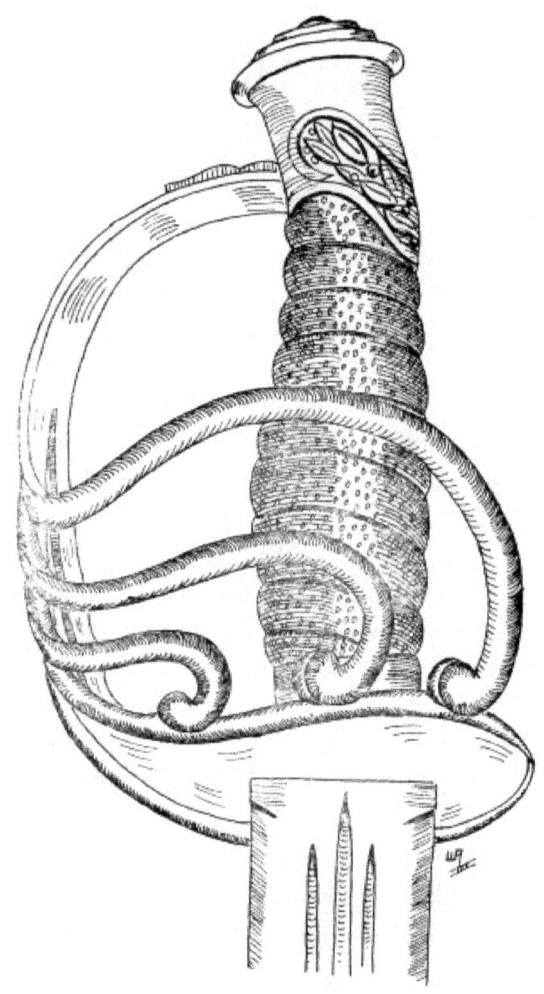

Plate 16

SIXTEEN
Gen. Wade Hampton's Sword

This sword is of French manufacture, but it is included because it is a type which is peculiarly identified with Wade Hampton. The Confederate Museum in Richmond, contains four such swords all identical except for minor details. Two of these swords were the personal property of Gen. Hampton, one was given by him to Gen. Bradley T. Johnson, C.S.A. of Maryland, and the fourth was given by him to Gen. M.C. Butler, C.S.A.. In each case the blades look older than the hilts and it is possible that Gen. Hampton secured the blades from one point, and had them rehilted. Wells in his *Hampton and his Cavalry* says: "At Columbia were made the heavy long straight double-edged swords, very serviceable and crusader-like with cross hilts." He must have been referring to these swords, and confused as to the type of guard.

This formidable weapon has an over-all length of 45 inches. The blade is double-edged 38 inches in length, 1 9/16-inch wide, with three deep channels in the middle of either side. The guard is of cast brass, and, with its four branches instead of the customary three, is very similar to the French Napoleonic dragoon sword. The grip is wrapped with sharkskin and wound with nine turns of single strand, and double strand brass wire. The pommel is decorated on the obverse as shown, and on the reverse with oak leaves and acorns. The scabbard is of metal with brass throat and toe, and two brass ring mounts. The blade was once etched but through wear the decorations are almost indistinguishable, although a French liberty cap, floral designs, and crossed cannons can be made out.

The swords of Gen. Butler and Gen. Johnson have leather grips, and leather scabbards, but are otherwise the same. The markings on those blades are also undecipherable.

The inside of the guard is equipped with a leather strap in which to insert the forefinger, giving a firmer hold on the grip.

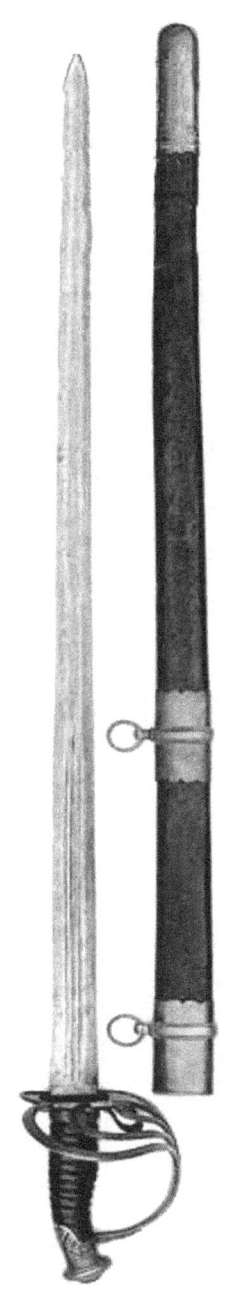

The sword of Gen. Wade Hampton.

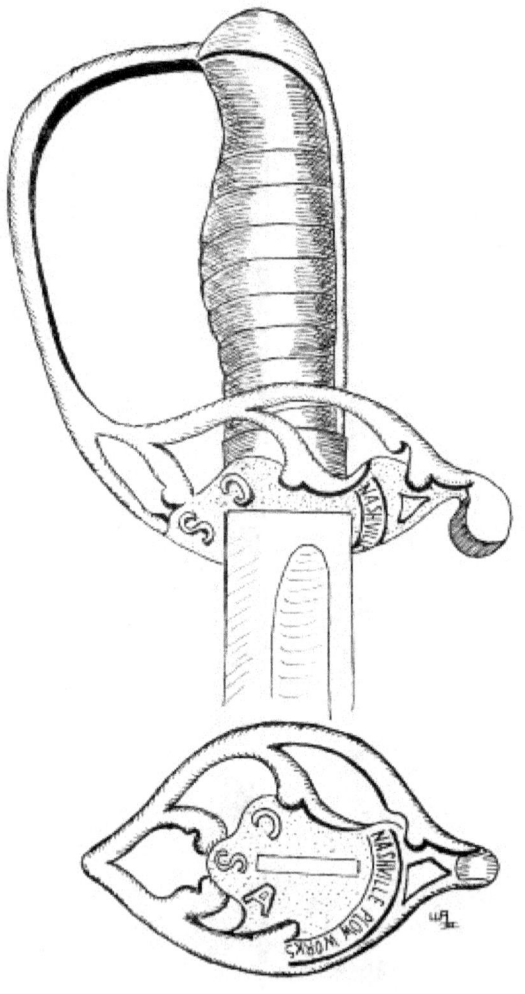

Plate 17

SEVENTEEN
Nashville Plow Works
Nashville, Tenn.

The goodly weapon pictured on the opposite page is part of the Battle Abbey collection, and was made by the Nashville Plow Works, of Nashville, Tenn., Sharp and Hamilton, owners.

Before the war, this firm operating under the same name manufactured all types of agricultural implements, but with the event of hostilities between the North and South, reversed the Biblical injunction, and proceeded to turn plow shards into swords.

Their sword-making activities were terminated abruptly with the fall of Nashville in April, 1862, at which time the plant was destroyed, and the owners cast into prison. The *Nashville Banner* of April 1, 1862, says: "Yesterday, Messrs. Sharp and Hamilton of the Nashville Plow Works were also arrested and put under bond of $3000 each for their appearance. The charge against these gentlemen is treason." But even for this brief period of time they must have made a large number of swords, judging from the large number which have survived. As far as is known, only cavalry sabres have been found bearing their name.

The sabre pictured has a 35-inch blade, curved, and with tapering blood gutter on either side. It is 1 1/4 inches wide with a flat back. The guard is of roughly cast brass containing the maker's name, as well as C.S.A., in large capital letters. The grip is of brown leather wound with ten turns of double stranded copper wire. The back strap is of brass with a metal collar at the base of the grip. Scabbard is of metal with brass ring mounts, throat and toe.

EIGHTEEN
L. T. Cunningham College Hill Arsenal
Nashville, Tenn.

Although the factory of the Nashville Plow Works was destroyed when the Federals occupied Nashville, evidently some of their equipment escaped destruction, as a number of swords of the same distinctive design have been found with the name Nashville Plow Works deleted. Comparison of these swords reveals the castings are identical, and probably made from the same pattern.

The Battle Abbey collection has a sword of this type without the name of the Nashville Plow Works. Inscribed on the blade is "J. W. Head, Col. 30th Tenn. Reg.," and what appears to be the maker's name, "L. T. Cunningham."

L. T. Cunningham operated in Nashville, where he was connected with the College Hill Arsenal. It is possible that Mr. Cunningham made no swords at all, and was only the agent, purchasing his swords through the Nashville Plow Works. Another possibility is that he made the blades, and purchased only the hilts from Sharp and Hamilton, operators of the Nashville Plow Works. In either event, in all probability, the name would have been deleted, as shown in the pictured sword (Plate 18, next page).

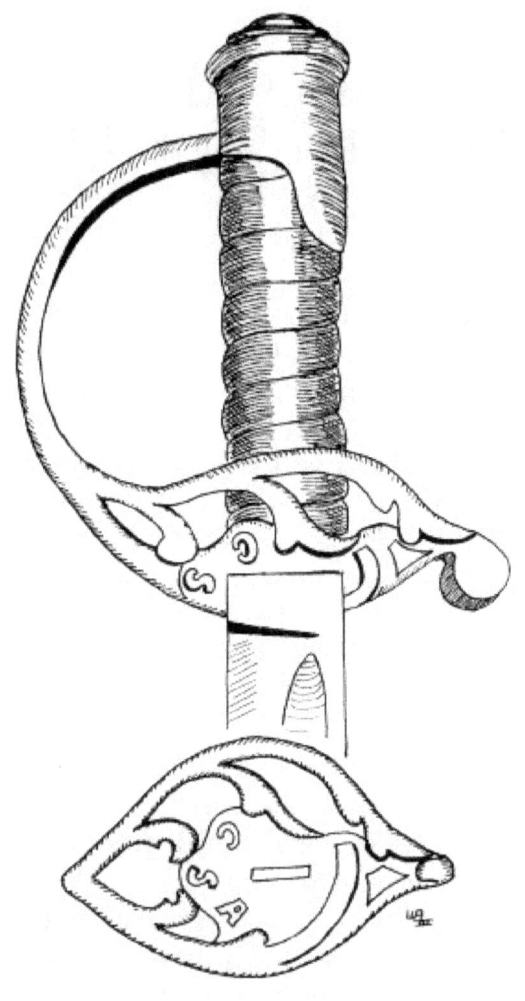

Plate 18

This is an officer's sword, of much better finish than those done by the Nashville Plow Works. The blade is 31 1/8 inches long, almost straight, 15/16 inch wide, flat on the back, with a shallow blood gutter of both sides. It is nicely etched with trophies, Confederate flag, and large letters "C.S.A." The knuckle guard describes a perfect half circle rather than the customary half oval, and also note the high pommel. The grip is of brown leather, wound with nine turns of double stranded brass wire. The guard is identical with that of the Nashville Plow Works, except that this name has been deleted. Sword has no back strap. Note the difference in the blade as compared with that of the Nashville Plow Works. The blade shows evidence of having been sharpened.

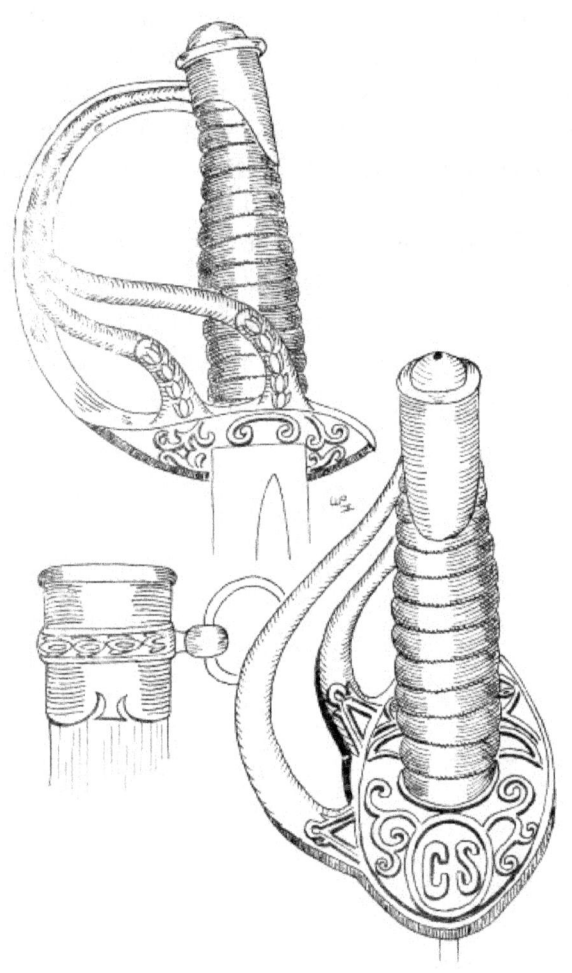

Plate 19

NINETEEN
Memphis Novelty Works
Thomas Leech & Co.
Memphis, Tenn.

The Memphis Novelty Works of Memphis, Tenn., turned out a quantity of swords for the Confederacy, a number of which have survived.

The sabre, whose hilt is shown, is in the Georgia Room of the Confederate Museum in Richmond, Va., and was presented to Col. George W. Raines, C.S.A., in charge of the powder works at Augusta, Ga., by the Memphis Novelty Works. It has a 30-inch blade with a decided curve, 11/16 inches wide with shallow blood gutter on either side. The grip is of leather wound with twelve turns of two stranded double twisted brass wire. The guard is of cast brass, of the three-branch variety, but highly decorated, as shown, and with the large letters "C.S." on the top of the guard inside an oval. The pommel is undecorated. The scabbard is of polished metal with three brass mounts.

Another sword by the same firm in the Battle Abbey collection has a long straight, double-edged blade, 36 inches long, leather, wire-wound grip, and brass guard. The scabbard is of metal, with brass bands and tip. On the brass guard is stamped: "Memphis Novelty Works, Thos. Leech & Co."

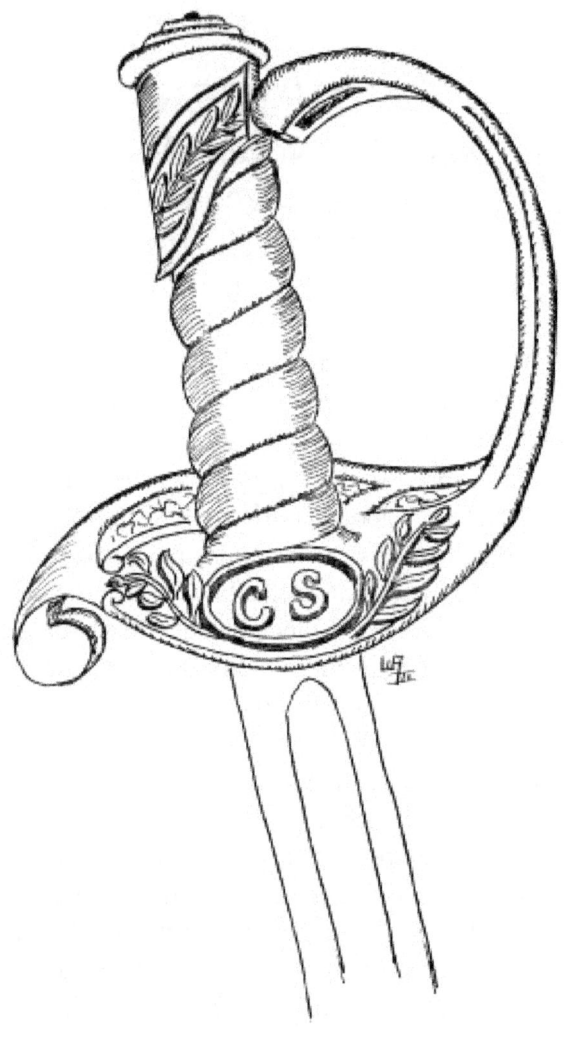

Plate 20

TWENTY
Memphis Novelty Works (continued)

In 1861, Thomas Leech, a cotton broker, through patriotism, or perhaps for gain, organized the Memphis Novelty Works, Thomas Leech & Company. The purpose of this company was to manufacture swords. It was located in Memphis, Tennessee, at Main and McCall Streets. In early '62, Charles H. Rigdon, became connected with the firm. Rigdon, a mechanical genius, was from St. Louis, Missouri, where he had associated with Dimick, and Shawk and McLanahan, all makers of imitation Colts.

Just before the fall of Memphis, on May 9, 1862, the Memphis Novelty Works removed to Columbus, Mississippi, where they operated until December 1862, when the approach of the Yankees again caused them to remove to Greensboro, Georgia. At this latter point they set up business at Bush and South Streets.

It is generally believed that up until this point they were engaged solely in sword making, although it is possible they also made a few revolvers. At any rate, on March 6, 1863, they secured a contract with the Confederate Government, to manufacture revolvers, and that their entire attention was turned to this line after this date, is shown by the sale of all sword making equipment on April 21, 1863. After this date the firm changed its name to Leech & Rigdon, and the partnership continued until December 13, 1863, when it was formally dissolved. Leech remained in Greensboro, supposedly continuing his revolver making while Rigdon went on to Augusta, Georgia, where he made the familiar Rigdon-Ansley 12 stop imitation Colts.

Pictured is another product of the Memphis Novelty Works, this example now part of the Battle Abbey collection. The blade is entirely without markings, and contains the single shallow groove on either side which for some reason has always been more or less a distinguishing feature of Confederate swords.

Although the maker's name does not appear, the distinctive design of the "C.S." in an oval on the guard identifies the manufacturer.

Leech and Rigdon Field Staff Sword - Memphis Novelty Works

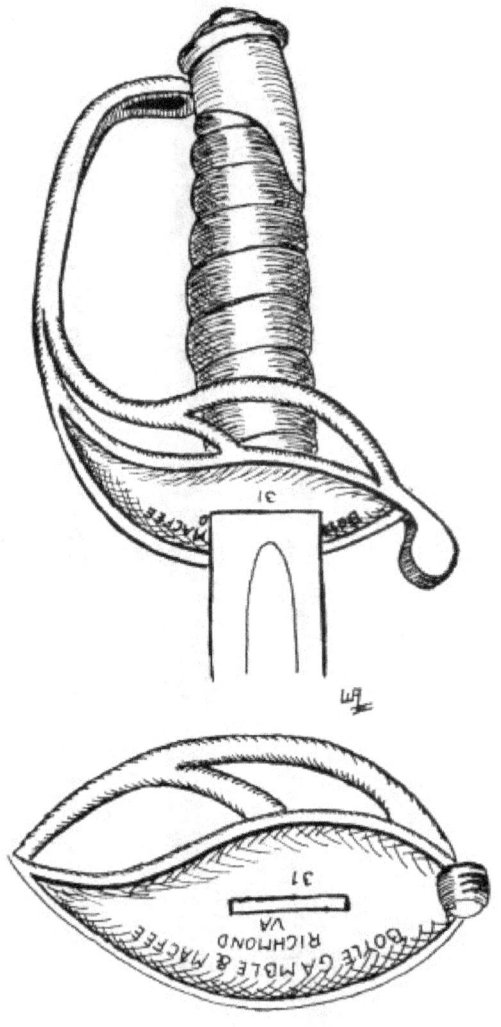

Plate 21

TWENTY-ONE
Boyle Gamble and MacFee
Richmond, Va.

Boyle Gamble & MacFee operated a sword factory in Richmond, Va., during the war years, and was located at the foot of S. 7th St., near the Tredegar Iron Works, and the Virginia Armory. There they made all types of swords, sabres, and bayonets.

The pictured sword has a distinctive guard which is peculiar to this firm, and while many of their weapons were marked with their name or initials, some appear totally without any mark of identification.

The blade is 29 5/8 inches long, 1 3/16 inches wide, with flat back, and tapered blood gutter on either side. The blade is almost straight and is unmarked. The grip is of leather wound with seventeen turns of single stranded copper wire. The guard more or less conforms to the foot officer's model, but with open spaces in the counterguard instead of the usual rose design. Cast in raised letters on the underside of the guard is the maker's name: "Boyle Gamble & MacFee, Richmond, Va." The pommel is undecorated. The number 31, appears on the underside of the guard, and on the pommel. The scabbard is of black leather with three brass mounts. Two swords of this type are to be found in the Battle Abbey collection.

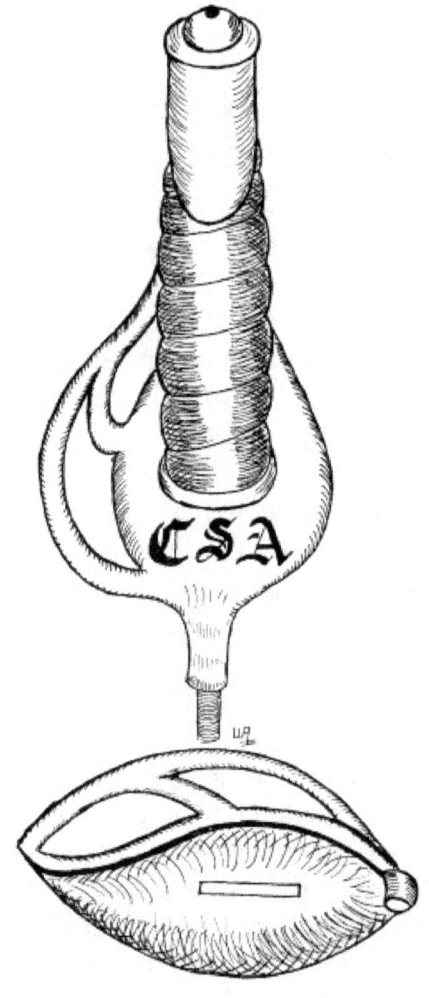

Plate 22

TWENTY-TWO
Boyle Gamble and MacFee (continued)

This is another sword by the above firm, which, however, does not bear the maker's name. Comparison with the sword in the preceding page will show that with the exception of the deleted name, the guards are identical.

The blade is 31 inches long, 1 inch wide, straight, with rounded back, and shallow blood gutter on either side. The grip is of leather wound with ten turns of single strand copper wire. On the top of the guard in old English letters is engraved "C.S.A."

This firm also made short swords, with a short cross arm guard, with the name "Boyle Gamble & MacFee" cast in raised letters on the face of the guard.

A bayonet made by this firm, is now in the Battle Abbey collection.

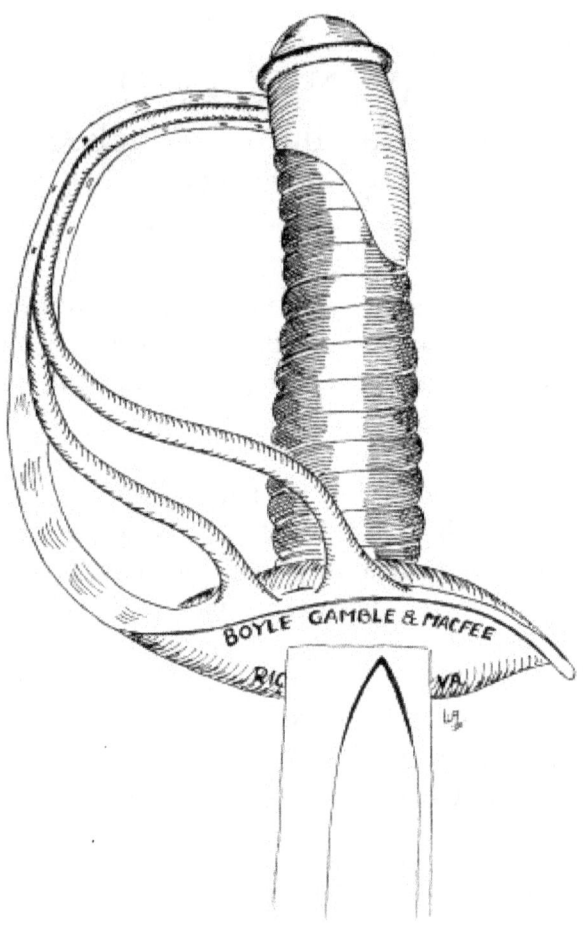

Plate 23

TWENTY-THREE
Boyle Gamble and MacFee (continued)

A Cavalry sabre which was carried by Capt. William Storke, of the Engineer Corps, C.S.A. is now in the possession of the Virginia Historical Society, in Richmond, Va.

This sabre has a blade 35 inches long, 1 1/4 inches wide, has a flat back, and is curved. A wide blood gutter extends on either side of the blade for a distance of 28 inches. The grip is of black leather wound with 17 turns of heavy single stranded copper wire. The guard, while of the three branch variety, nevertheless with its inverted saucer shape conforms to the style set by this firm in their foot officer's swords. On the underside of the guard is cast in raised letters "Boyle Gamble & MacFee, Richmond, Va.," but note that comparison with the foot sword shown in Plate 21, reveals the "Richmond, Va.," to be in a different position.

The weapon has a 40 1/2-inch over-all length, and has a metal scabbard with two brass ring mounts.

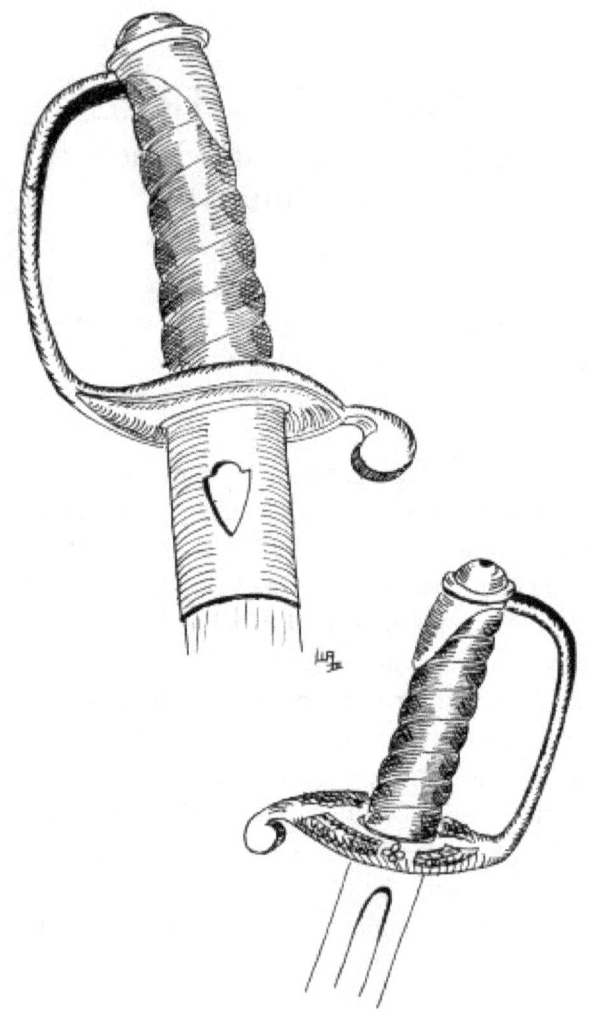

Plate 24

TWENTY-FOUR
Boyle Gamble & MacFee
(continued)

On the opposite page is pictured a sword which might possibly have been made by the above firm, and which is unquestionably Confederate. Note that the pommel is identical with those swords just preceding, and the No. 2 which appears on the top of the pommel, and on the knuckle guard where it joins the pommel, has been stamped in the same fashion and place where I have seen others stamped, which were marked with this maker's name.

This is evidently a non-commissioned officer's sword, or possibly an artillery officer's sword. There is a crude attempt at decoration on the guard which is of cast brass, and which resembles other swords made by Boyle Gamble & MacFee. The blade is straight, 24 inches long, with rounded back, and tapering blood gutters on both sides. The grip is of black leather wound with single strand brass wire. The scabbard is of black leather with brass throat and toe.

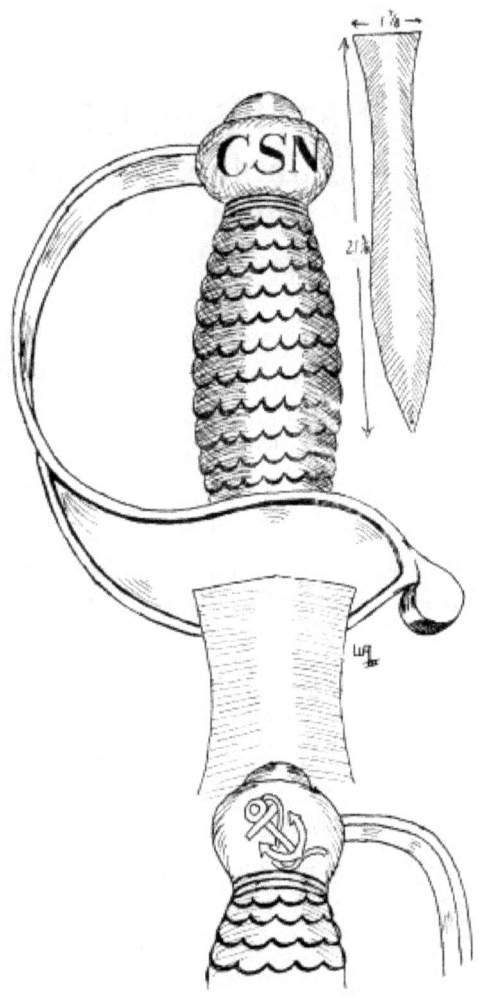

Plate 25

TWENTY-FIVE
Confederate Naval Cutlass

Confederate Navy cutlasses as a rule were modeled after the obsolete type used in the United States Navy in the Mexican War. The pictured sword is believed to have been made in Richmond, Va. The blade is double-edged, 21 3/8 inches long, 1 7/8 inches wide with a diamond cross section. Over-all length is 27 inches. Grip and guard are of cast brass, the grip in imitation of fish scales. Cast into the obverse of the pommel are the large letters "CSN" and on the reverse a fouled anchor. The scabbard is of leather and the frog and belt are of cotton webbing with leather mounts. The belt is fastened with a small hook in place of a buckle.

This weapon is part of the Battle Abbey collection. If the hilt is unseated from the blade of these swords, a small capital "W" will be found stamped on both guard and grip. The meaning of this mark is not known, although it might be well to state that on almost every Confederate sword that has been unseated the author has found several cryptic marks such as dots, series of dots, scratches, Roman numerals, etc.

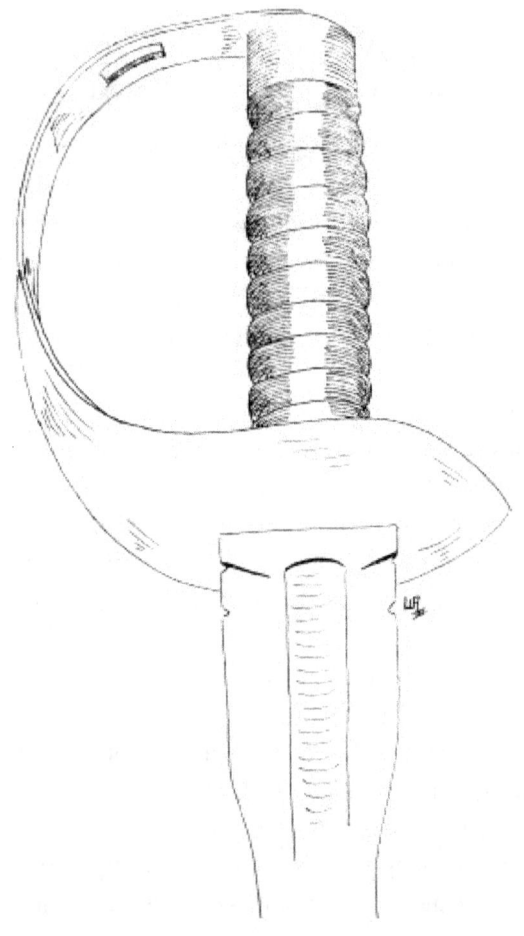

Plate 26

TWENTY-SIX
Tredegar Iron Works
Richmond, Va.

In the Virginia Room at the Confederate Museum, is a sword which was made at the Tredegar Iron Works in Richmond, and presented to the Museum by Gen. Charles J. Anderson, C.S.A., one of the owners.

The blade of this unusual piece is 28 3/4 inches long, 1 1/2 inches wide at the hilt, and 9 1/2 inches from the hilt tapers rapidly to 1 inch. A blood gutter runs down the center of the blade. The general appearance of the double-edged blade is that of a colichemarde. The grip is of turned wood which has ten parallel grooves. The guard is made of sheet metal, and is 3 3/8 inches wide. The pommel is a plain metal cap. There is a slot in the knuckle guard for a sabre-tasche.

The sword has no identifying marks.

The Tredegar Iron Works, contained the only rolling mill in the South at the start of the war. All types of munitions, and military equipment were made there. The Iron Works, was located just west of the Virginia Armory in Richmond, in the old Kenawha canal.

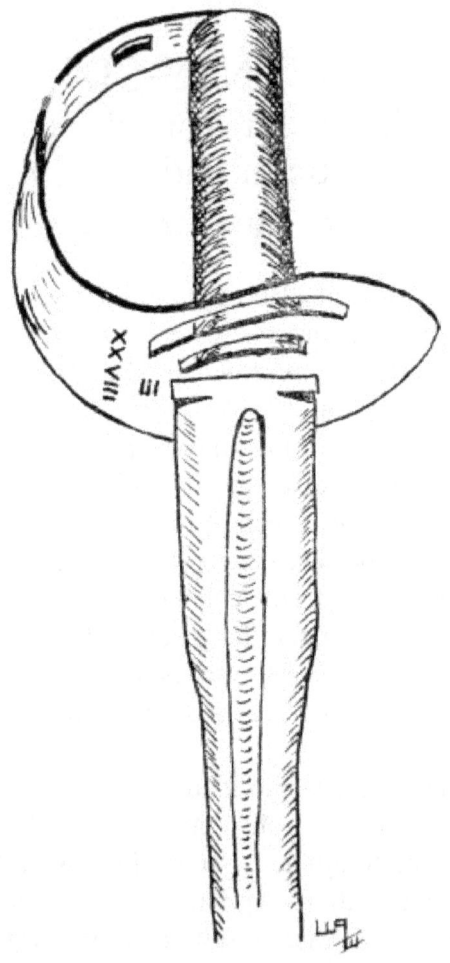

Plate 27

TWENTY-SEVEN
Tredegar Iron Works (continued)

      This pictured sword is almost identical with the one just preceding, and has identical measurements. It has, however, pieced slots in the counterguard, and the blood gutter is deeper, and does not extend up to the hilt. The grip of this sword is of metal, which apparently is a repair job, and the original grip must have been similar to the sword just described. The Roman numerals "XXVIII" and "III" are stamped on the underside of the guard.

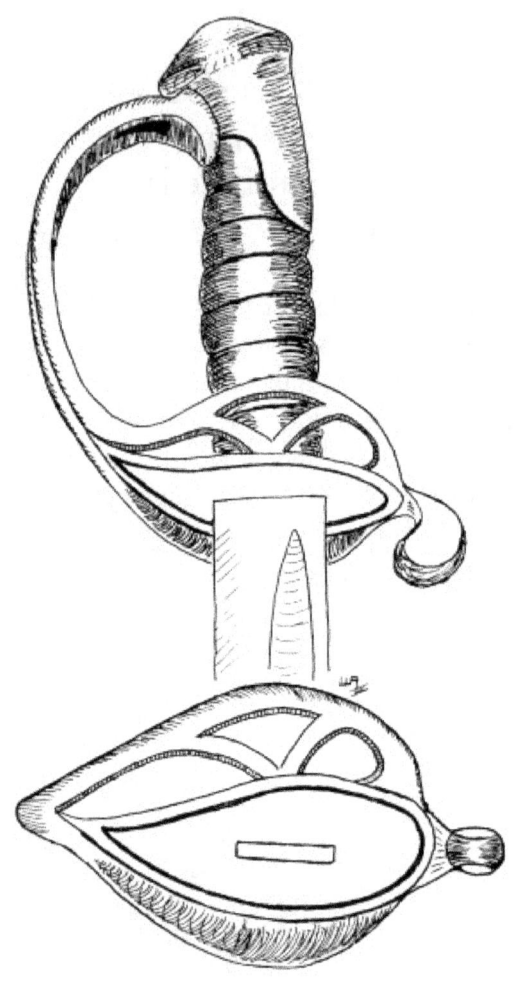

Plate 28

TWENTY-EIGHT
Virginia Armory
Richmond, Va.

The Virginia armory was established in Richmond, Va., in 1797, and served Virginia faithfully through all the following wars, until destroyed in the evacuation of Richmond, in April, 1865. Various types of guns, rifles, pistols, swords, and sabres, were made and repaired there.

In the Confederate Museum in Richmond, Va., is the sword pictured on the opposite page, which was worn by Maxwell T. Clarke, Lieutenant, C.S.N., during the last three years of the war. This sword was made by the Virginia Armory, and is in the Virginia Room in the museum. The blade is almost straight, 30 inches long, 1 inch wide, with tapering blood gutter on either side. It is frosted with floral designs, crossed cannons, crossed lances, and on the reverse near the hilt are the small letters "C.S.A." formed in a triangle. The guard is of cast brass conforming to the foot officer's model, but with open spaces in the counter-guard instead of the customary rose design. The pommel is heavy and undecorated. The grip is covered with black leather wound with ten turns of single stranded brass wire. The weapon has a leather scabbard with three brass mounts. Over-all length is 35 inches.

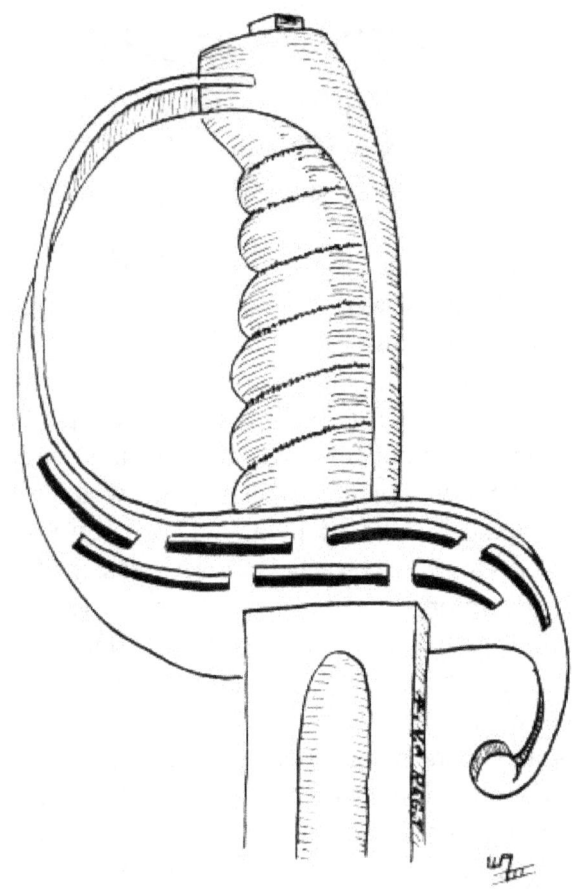

Plate 29

TWENTY-NINE
Virginia Manufactory Sabres
Richmond, Va.

Long known among collectors as "Hession Sabres," these swords are now generally identified as products of the Richmond Armory, or Virginia Manufactory.

These swords were all made in the early part of the 19th century, and all conform more or less to the same general pattern as to iron-pierced guards. The cavalry sabres carried a 40-inch scimitar blade, deadly in appearance, but undoubtedly very awkward as to actual use. The artillery sabres were not so curved, and had blades only 35 inches in length.

From about 1820, until 1861, these sabres were stored in various arsenals and armories over the State. The scarcity of arms in 1861 again called these swords into service, and they were issued to Virginia troopers, but were found by them to be so cumbersome that hundreds were recalled and shortened to 35-inch blade, and were then rescabbarded, the new scabbards being of iron with brass mounts.

Practically all Virginia Manufactory sabres are stamped either "1st Va. Regt." or "4th Va. Regt.," on the back of the blade. Some contain serial numbers, while others are totally without markings.

The Battle Abbey collection has No. 1, the 40-inch blade as originally made; No. 2, another sword of this same type but with blade shortened to 35 inches for Confederate use; and No. 3, an artillery sabre of early 1800's, as originally made with blade of 35 inches.

THIRTY
Confederate Foot Officer's Sword

The theory has been advanced that all the hilts were made by one firm who sold them to various blade manufacturers, and certainly the wide variance in blades would indicate that this might be true. They are found with elaborately etched blades and some without any etching at all. The hilts all have a number stamped on the underside of the guard.

A sword of this type is in the Confederate Museum in Richmond, with elaborately etched blade showing Confederate flags, a picture of Jeff Davis, and "CSA" on the blade. On the hilt is stamped "5."

Another sword of this type with sharkskin grip has the following inscription on the blade: "Presented to Lieut. Col. C.G. Coleman, of the 23rd Reg. Va. Vols. by his friends in Co. 'G,' April 22, 1862." Near the hilt was also etched: "made for Mitchell & Tyler, Richmond, Va." Mitchell and Tyler, were a well-known jewelry firm in Richmond during the war, and their name appears on buttons, and other military equipment, but they were not manufacturers.

The pictured sword (Plate 30, next page) has an over-all length of 37 inches, with a 31-inch blade, 1 inch

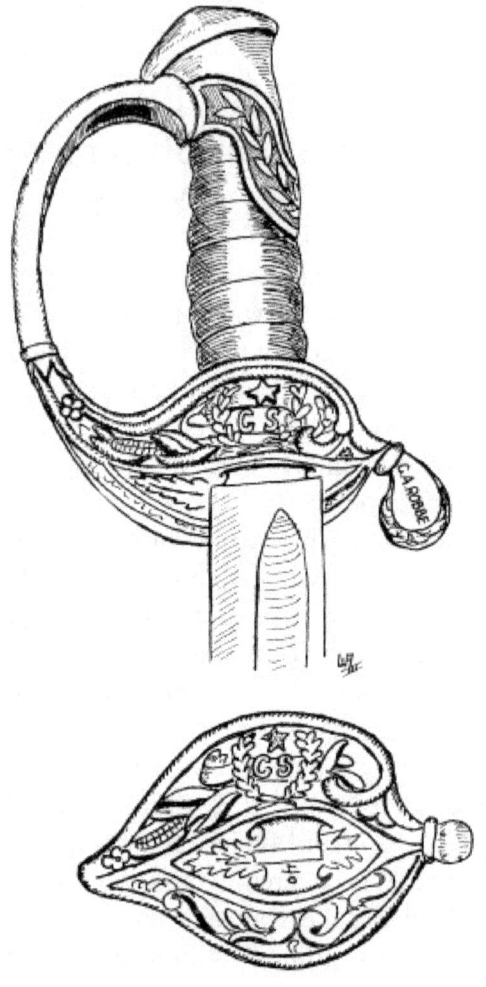

Plate 30

wide. The blade has a rounded back, and a shallow blood gutter on either side. It is etched with floral designs, flags, and a shield containing the letters "CSA." The hilt is of brass, and the counterguard contains an ear of corn, a wreath surmounted by a star, and the letters "CS" on a ribbon inside the wreath. The number "13" is stamped on the underside of the guard, and the name "C. A. Robbe" is stamped on the reverse of the quillon. His name does not appear in Confederate Archives, but certainly he is not the maker. The grip is of leather wound with seven turns of single strand brass wire. The scabbard is of leather with brass mounts.

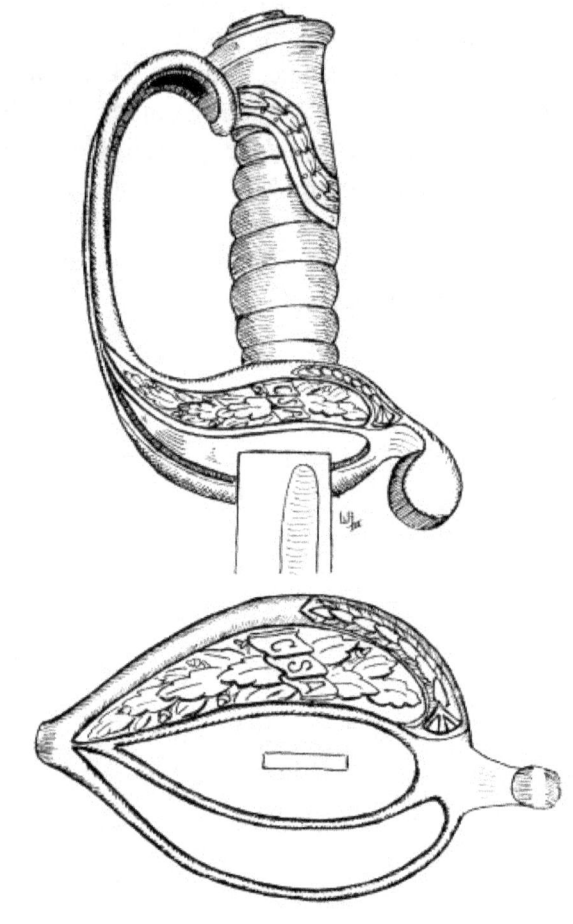

Plate 31

THIRTY-ONE
Confederate Foot Officer's Sword (continued)

    This type of infantry officer's sword is quite rare, and gives no clue to the identity of its maker.

    The blade is almost straight, 30 inches long, 15/16 inches wide with a rounded back and a shallow blood gutter on either side. Over-all length is 35 inches. The guard is of cast brass, the counterguard having a design of oak leaves on which is superimposed a ribbon bearing the small letters "C.S.A." The pommel is decorated with oak leaves. The grip is of leather wound with twelve turns of single stranded copper wire. Roman numerals are cut in the end of the quillon and on the brass throat of the metal scabbard, with brass rings and toe. The scabbard is painted a deep red.

    The specimen in the Battle Abbey has the numeral "VI."

    In many years of collecting only three such swords have come to the writer's attention.

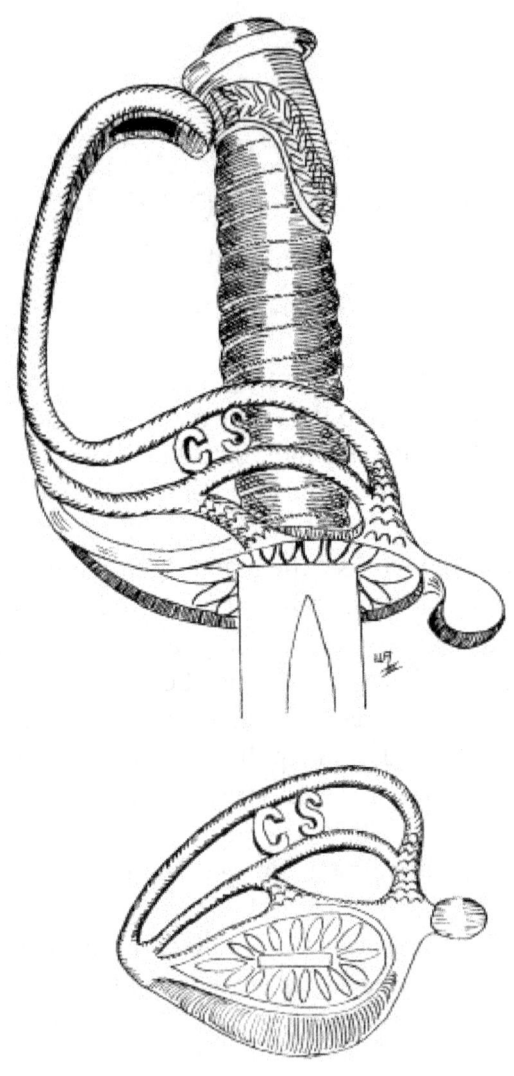

Plate 32

THIRTY-TWO
Confederate Field Officer's Sword

Except for the number "290" which is stamped on the blade, and on the underside of the guard, no clue appears on this weapon as to its manufacturer. These swords are not common.

The blade is almost straight, 32 inches long, with wide shallow groove on either side. The over-all length is 38 1/2 inches. Top of the blade is flat. Blade shows evidence of having been sharpened. The guard is of nicely cast brass with large letters "CS" between the branches. Grip of brown leather wound with fifteen turns of double stranded brass wire. Pommel decorated with leaf design.

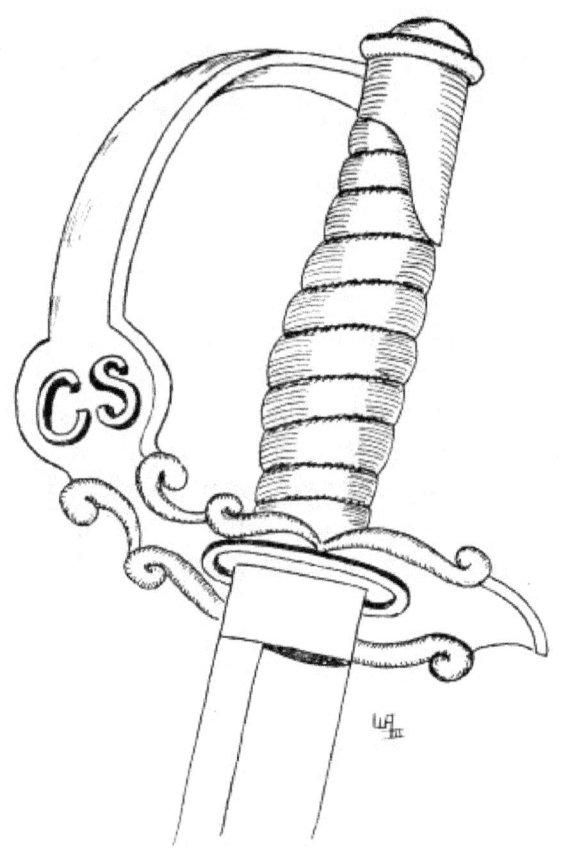

Plate 33

THIRTY-THREE
Confederate Artillery (?) Sabre

This sword is part of the Battle Abbey Collection, and is the only sword of this type that has come to our attention. Where they were made and by whom is not known.

The guard which contains the raised cast letters "C.S." is definitely of artillery type, and yet the blade conforms to calvary, and has a stopped blood gutter, which is unusual in a Confederate. The scabbard is typically Confederate in that it is of metal with brass ring mounts. With such great diversity of equipment and arms which existed throughout the Confederacy, this writer has always wondered at the two general points on which Confederate swords usually conform – 1st, distinguishing feature is that most contained the unstopped blood gutter, and 2nd, the metal scabbards usually bore brass ring mounts. It is supposed that the cause of these two features is due in each case to the lack of skilled armorers, as obviously a shallow groove, was easier to beat into a sword than a stopped blade, and of course brass was easier to work than iron or steel in making a ring mount. However, this principle seemed to apply even in the case of some of the exceptionally handsome swords that were turned out by men who very obviously were skilled in this particular art.

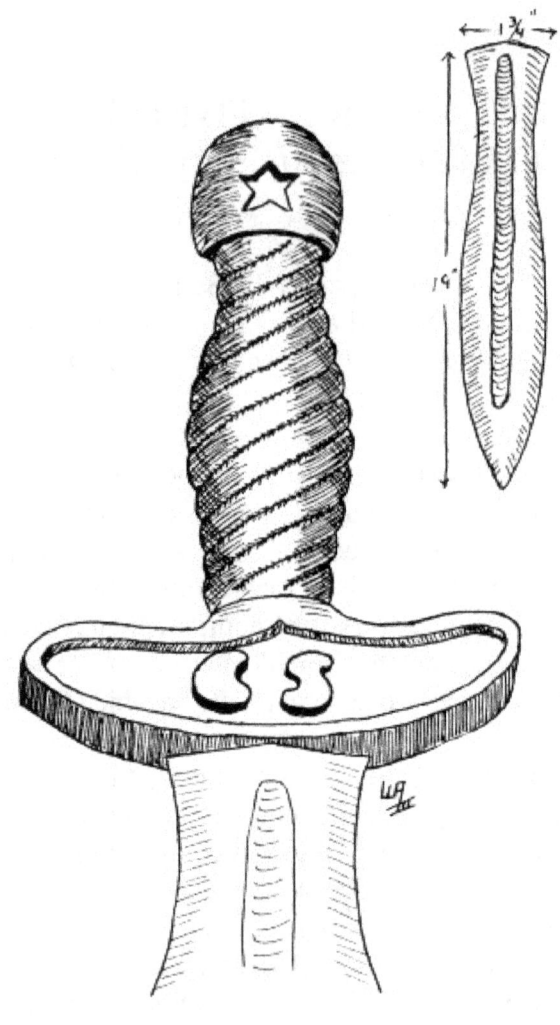

Plate 34

THIRTY-FOUR
Confederate Short Sword

This is one of the most familiar of all Confederate weapons.

The sword is roughly patterned after the short artillery sword turned out by the thousands by Ames & Co., until 1859. The hilt is of poorly cast brass, very heavy, with short cross arm guard, in which the raised letters "C.S." are cast on either side. A star is cast on both sides of the pommel. The blade is 19 inches long, 2 inches wide, double-edged, with a deep channeling in the center of both sides. Over-all length is 24 1/2 inches. The scabbard is of black leather with two brass mounts.

While some collectors are of the opinion that the star signifies the weapon was made in Texas, or for Texans, nothing has ever been brought forth to prove this theory, and those examined were totally devoid of any mark which might give a clue as to its maker. Some collectors are of the opinion that these are the product of L. Haiman & Bro.

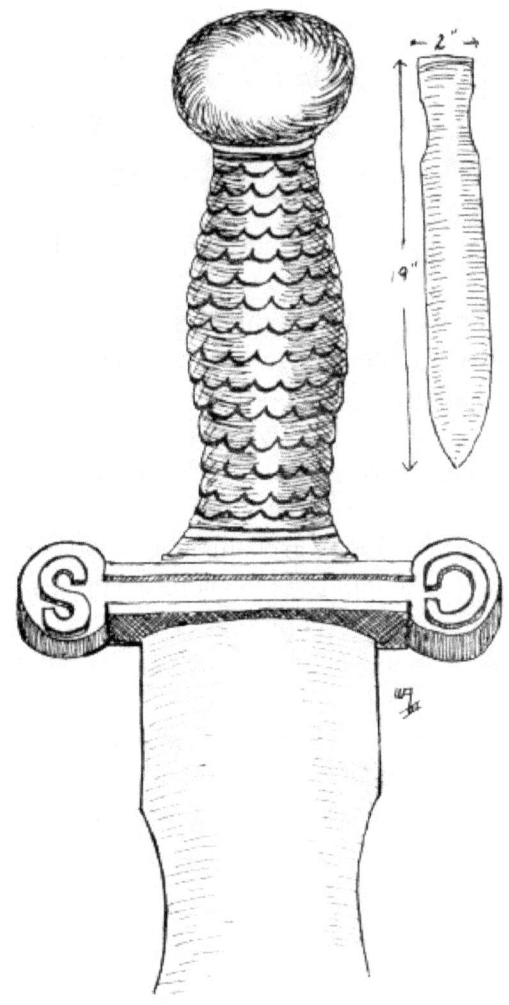

Plate 35

THIRTY-FIVE
Short Artillery Sword (Foot)

About the most useless weapon made in the South, was the short sword for foot artillery modeled after the type used in the United States Army in the Mexican War, which had been adopted from the French type of 1830.

The Union Army used the foot artillery swords only in the first part of the war. That the Confederate Army ever used them seems open to argument, but the fact remains that thousands of them were made at several places.

In the Battle Abbey collection is one of these swords with wooden scabbard with iron mounts. The grip and hilt are of poorly cast brass or copper and the double-edged blade is 19 inches long. On the blade in small letters is stamped "C.S."

Another and similar weapon in this same collection has on the hilt in small letters "B. J. Johnson, Macon, Ga."

A third type of much better workmanship is pictured. It has a heavy double-edged blade, oval cross section with no channeling. Blade is 19 inches long, 2 inches wide, and 24 1/2 inches overall. The grip is of cast brass with eagle feather design. The guard is formed by a short cross arm which ends in a disk, the large letters "C" and "S" appearing in raised letters on opposite ends of the disk.

Another type rarely seen is that with the simulated eagle feather grip with large cast letters "C.S.A." on the cross arm guard. This is not to be confused with the crudely made sword pictured in Plate 34.

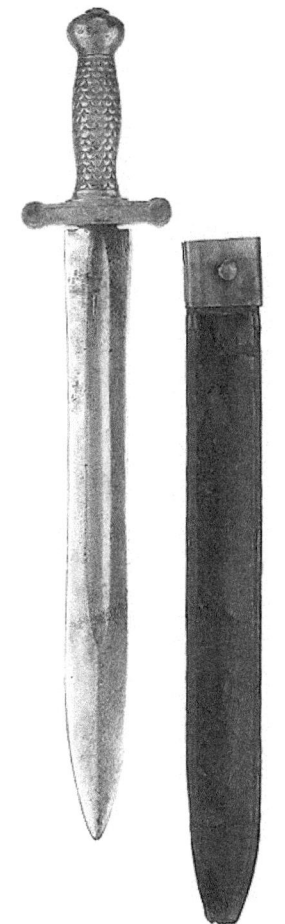

Short Confederate artillery sword.

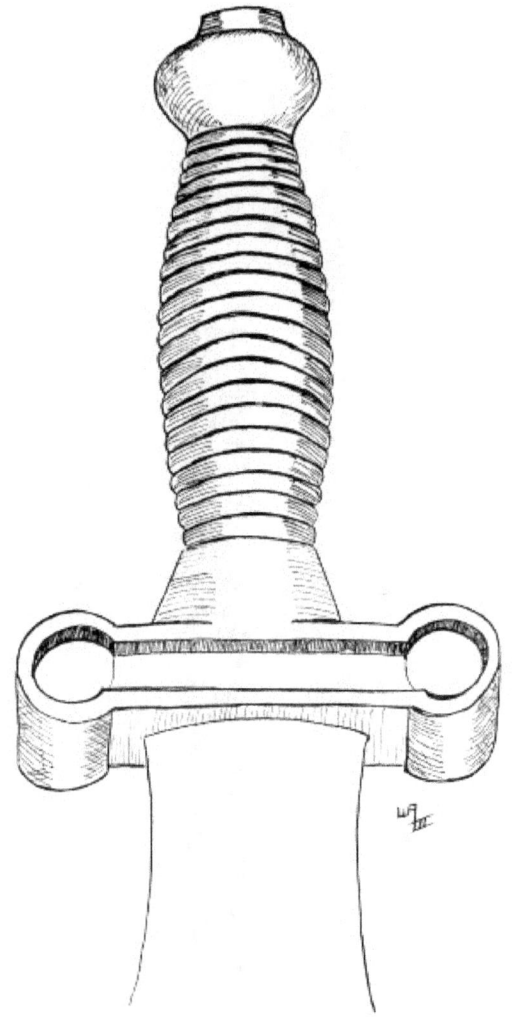

Plate 36

THIRTY-SIX
Short Artillery Sword (Foot)

The pictured sword is totally devoid of any markings, and can be identified only by the crudeness of workmanship. It is an imitation of the foot artillery sword used by the U.S. Army in the Mexican War, which was in turn copied from the French foot-artillery sword.

Swords similar to this were made apparently at a number of points in the South. As a weapon they were practically useless, but satisfied the desire held by the average Confederate soldier of having some sort of an edged weapon of any kind at all.

The pictured sword has a crudely cast brass guard, with 20-inch straight blade, no channeling, and oval cross section.

Swords of this type are still turning up with great regularity, and are one of the commonest of all Confederate weapons, which would indicate that literally thousands of them must have been made.

Scabbards for these swords were of leather with brass mounts, although some were evidently made with wooden scabbards.

Plate 37

THIRTY-SEVEN
Confederate Naval Cutlass

    This type of Naval cutlass is unique in that it has no hand guard and is identical in design with that of foot artillery swords.

    In the museum of the Chicago Historical Society is a hard wood pattern for this cutlass handle and hilt.

    On one side of the hilt are the letters "C.S.N." On the other side is a fouled anchor in raised design.

    The label attached to this pattern says that it was made by Frederick Heyer, of Richmond, and used by him in making the brass handles and hilts for this type of cutlass, but whether these weapons were made up at Tredegar Iron Works, or at the sword factory (Boyle Gamble & MacFee) in Richmond, is a matter of conjecture.

    Specimens of this type of cutlass are quite scarce. They are well made with 21 7/8-inch blades, 1 7/8 inches wide, with no grooves. Scabbards were of leather with brass mounts.

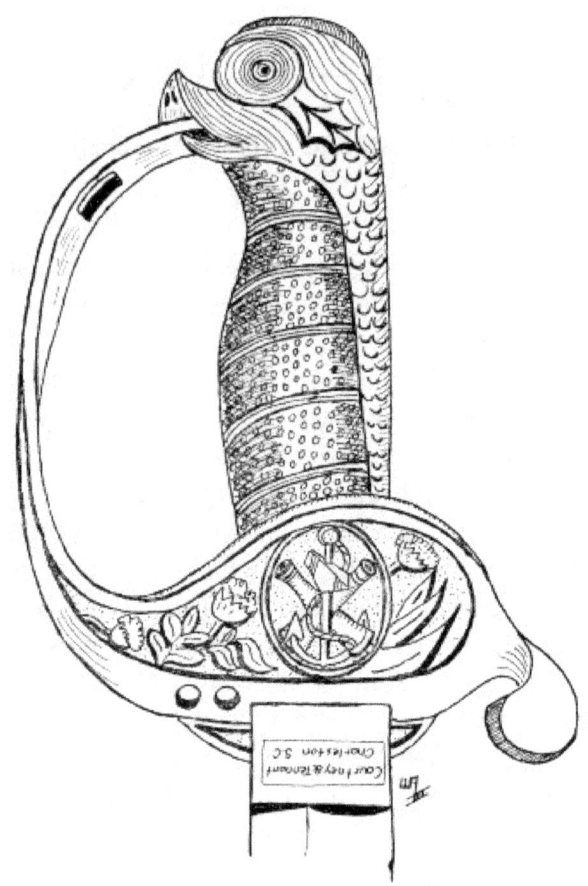

Plate 38

THIRTY-EIGHT
Robert Mole & Sons
Birmingham, England

The firm of Robert Mole & Sons of Birmingham, England, furnished the Confederacy with a number of fine swords.

A Confederate Naval officer's sword by this company is pictured. The blade is 29 inches long, 15/16 inches wide, is straight, and has a wide shallow groove on either side. The obverse is decorated in silver chasing with the Confederate Naval flag superimposed upon an anchor, and with designs of cotton and tobacco plants. The reverse is similarly decorated and bears the Confederate Naval Coat of Arms (crossed cannon superimposed upon a fouled anchor). Stamped on the blade near the hilt is "Courtney & Tennant, Charleston, S.C." The maker's name "Mole" is stamped on the back of the blade, and on the underside of the guard. The guard is of cast brass with the Confederal Naval Coat of Arms, tobacco leaves, and cotton plants in high relief in the counterguard. The reverse side of the counterguard is hinged. The backstrap, and pommel is formed in the shape of a sea monster. The grip is of sharkskin, wound with seven turns of three-stranded brass wire. The scabbard is of leather with three brass mounts, two of which are encircled by rings in the form of ropes. The brass tip of the scabbard is formed by two twisted fish.

The weapon is beautifully executed, and has an overall length of 34 1/2 inches.

The name of Courtney & Tennant is not the name of the maker as many persons suppose, but is the name of a large importing firm which operated in Charleston, S.C., during the war. Their name is frequently found on buttons, and other military equipment which they imported through the blockade, but they did no manufacturing.

A sword of this type is in the National Museum in Washington, D.C., and several examples are to be found in the Confederate Museum in Richmond, Va.

Cavalry sabre manufactured by Isaac's & Co., London.

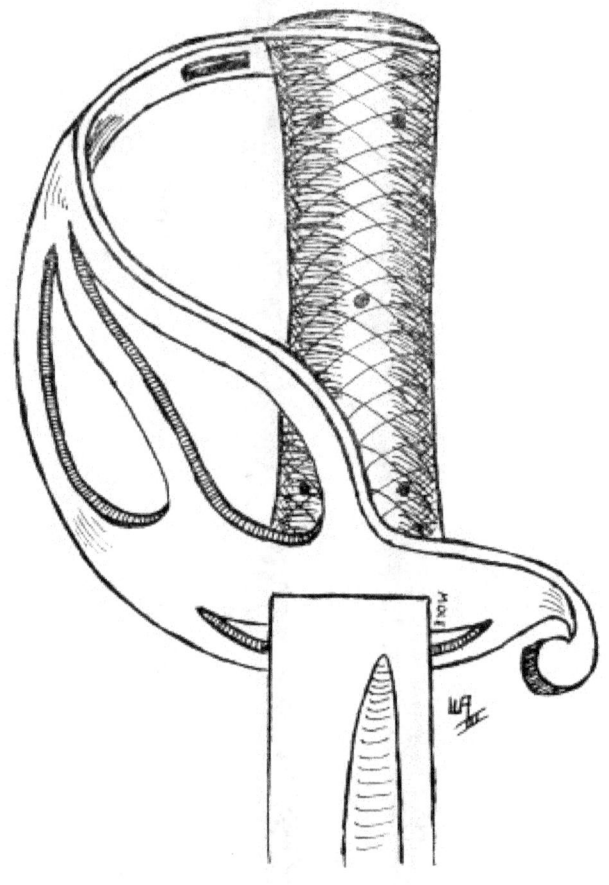

Plate 39

THIRTY-NINE
Robert Mole & Sons (continued)

The most familiar type sword by Mole is the one pictured on the opposite page. Swords of this type were sent into the South by the thousands through the blockade, and are better known as the "Enfield" type. While the brass guards are crude, the blades themselves are very good.

The blade is 34 1/2 inches long, with over-all length 39 3/4 inches, blade is 1 5/16 inches wide, almost straight, with wide shallow channeling on both sides. On the back of the blade, and on the underside of the guard is stamped "Mole." The grip is of checkered gutta-percha, riveted onto the tang of the blade. The guard is of cast brass, but gives the appearance of having been stamped from a sheet of plate brass. It has the regulation three branches, is very heavy and cumbersome-looking in appearance. The scabbard is of metal with iron ring mounts.

Swords of this same general pattern were also made by "Isaac's & Co." of London, the blades being identical with that described above, but stamped "Isaac's & Co." instead of "Mole." The guard, although of the same pattern, is of iron.

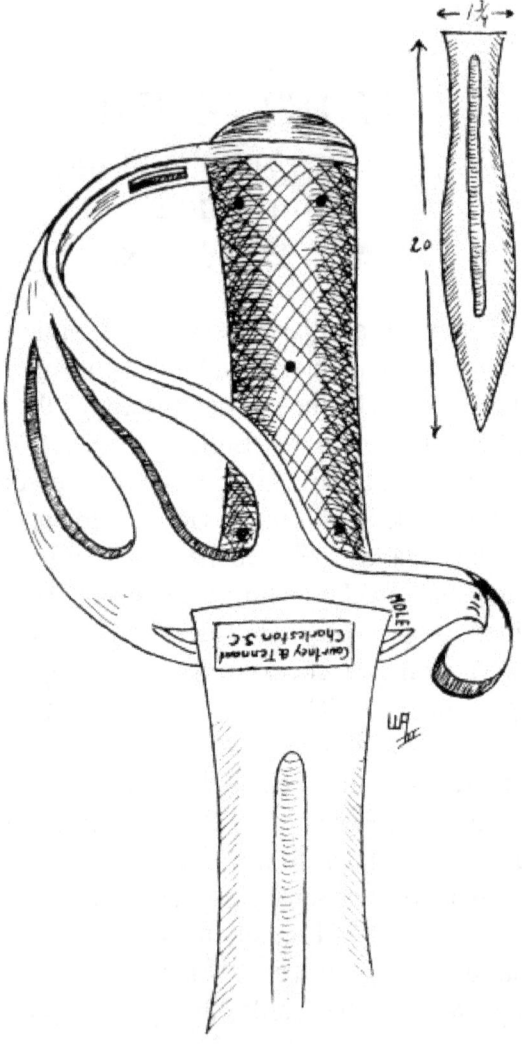

Plate 40

FORTY
Robert Mole & Sons (continued)

In addition to the naval officers' swords, and cavalry sabres, Robert Mole & Sons, also made Naval cutlasses, an example of which is pictured. A comparison with the preceding page will show that the brass guard, gutta-percha grip are identical with that of the cavalry sabre. The blade is double-edged 20 inches long, 1 3/4 inches wide. It is stamped on the back near the hilt "Mole." The same stamp appears on the underside of the guard. Also stamped on the blade is "Courtney & Tennant, Charleston, S.C.," which firm imported the sword but did not make it. The scabbard is of black leather with two brass mounts. Another sword seen, almost identical with the above, was one with a solid brass basket type of guard, rather than the three-branched one described. Otherwise it was the same, having the same type of blade with the same marking, and the same gutta-percha grip.

The naval officers' swords have an interesting documentary background. Commodore North, Confederate Navy Department agent in England, wrote on July 10, 1863: "The swords and buttons were gotten up with great care by Mr. G.B. Tennant of Courtney & Tennant, Charleston, S.C." (*Official Records: Navies*, Series II, Vol. II, p. 458).

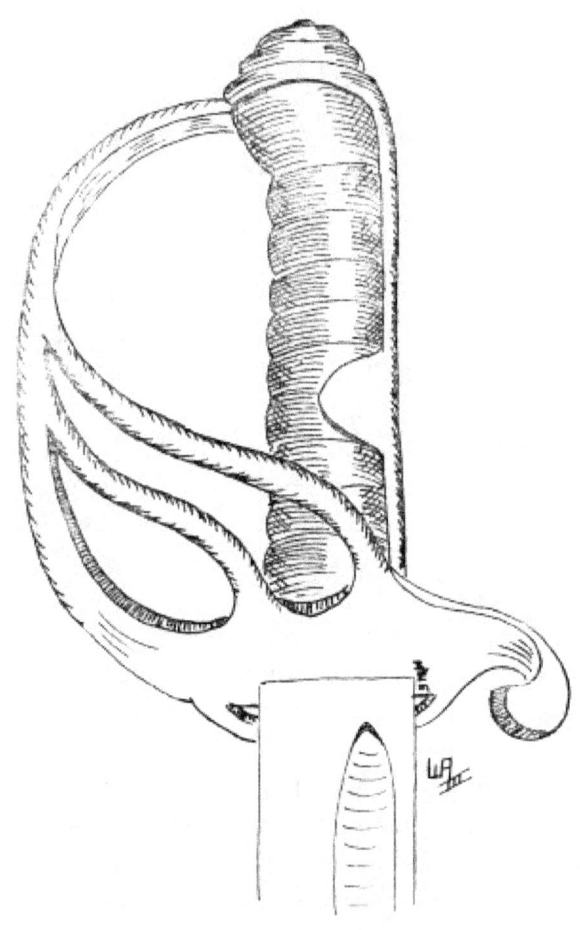

Plate 41

FORTY-ONE
Robert Mole & Sons (continued)

Here is pictured another sword by Robert Mole, obviously being an officer's sword. The blade is identical with that of the cavalry sabre already described.

The guard is patterned after the "Ames" Dragoon U.S. sabre of 1833-1840, and is of metal, not brass. Back strap, and button-type pommel are also of metal. Small shield extends on either side of the backstrap. Grip covered with leather, wound with wire.

Scabbard of metal with two metal ring mounts. The guard and top of blade stamped "Mole."

This is a Confederate officer's sword run in through the blockade.

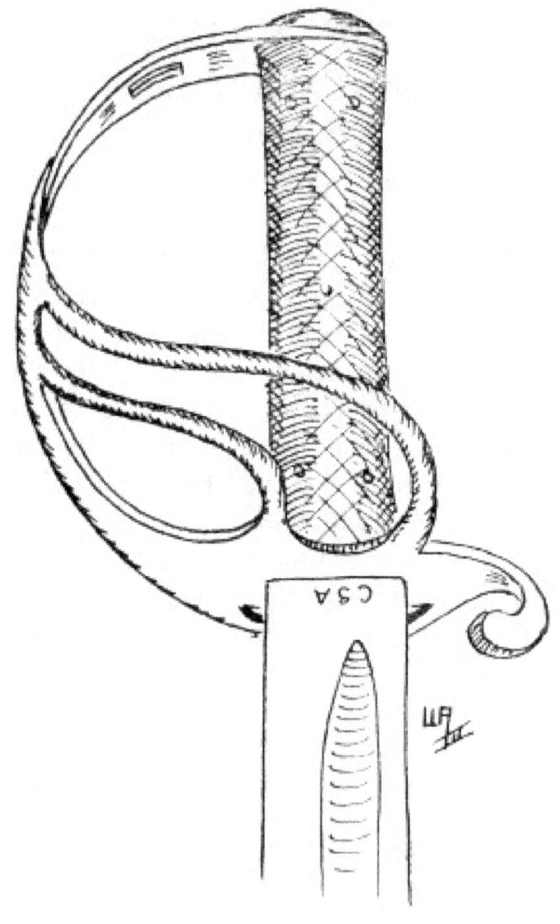

Plate 42

FORTY-TWO
Isaac's & Co.
☆ ☆ ☆ ☆

The pictured sword is a common type of Confederate cavalry sabre, made in England, and shipped to the South by the thousands through the blockade. Except for the guard which is iron, they are identical with those made by Robert Mole & Sons of Birmingham, England. The blade is almost straight, 34 1/2 inches long, 1 5/16 inches wide with shallow blood gutter on either side. On the top of the blade is stamped "Isaac's & Co." On the blade itself is stamped "C.S.A." The guard is of the three-branch variety of iron, not brass. The grip is of gutta-percha, identical with that of the "Mole" sabre. "C.S." is stamped on the top of the pommel. The scabbard is of metal with metal carrying rings. The scabbard is stamped "C.S.A."

The stampings in this case are genuine, and probably stamped at the time the sword was made. Similar swords are stamped "Va," "NC," evidently for the individual Southern States which contracted these swords at the start of the war. Confederate buttons which were marked on the back "S. Isaac's Campbell & Co., London," are very common.

On the following page, is described a sword made by the same firm. Some swords of this same type are without any markings whatsoever.

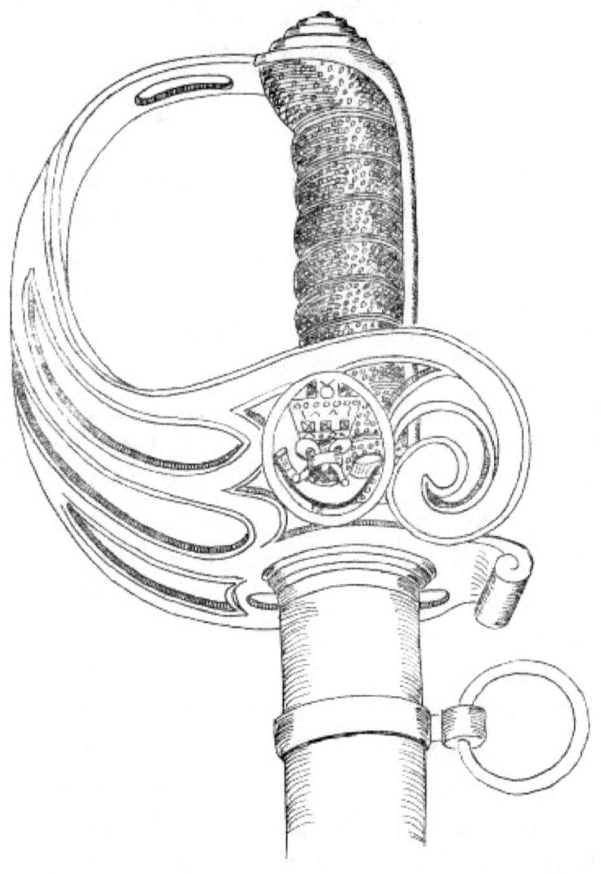

Plate 43

FORTY-THREE
S. Isaac's Campbell & Co.
St. Jermyn St., London, England

Another sabre of English manufacture, and made by the above firm, is in the National Museum in Washington, D.C., and was carried by Capt. William Wheeler, C.S.A. It has a long slender blade with slight curve and a diamond shaped point. Each side bears a medium-sized groove, and is etched with the figure of an eagle surmounted by eleven stars. The grip is covered with fish skin and wound with seven turns of copper wire. The top is covered with a convex metal plate, which terminates in a button-shaped pommel. The guard consists of a wide thin steel plate which widens into a broad counterguard at the blade. This plate is divided into four branches by open work, and bears at the blade in openwork, a crown surmounting a bugle. The blade is 83.5 cm long, 2.5 cm wide, with an over-all length of 97.7 cm. The blade is incribed S. Campbell & Co., St. Jermyn St., London.

I have seen swords of this same general type which have the letters "C.S." crudely marked in the counterguard by a series of small dots, and whose blades were etched with trophies, Confederate flags, and the letters "C.S.A."

Firmin of London, an old firm of military outfitters,

also made swords for the Confederacy.

In the Battle Abbey is a similar sword, the blade etched on each side with an eagle, a shield "C.S.A.," eleven stars and scroll work.

On the blade near the hilt is "Halfmann & Taylor, Montgomery, Alabama, and London." Also a brass disk set in the blade is "proved." On this sword instead of the crown and bugle is an oval plate in the counterguard which shows the eagle, with shield, eleven stars, and "C.S.A." crudely etched.

Halfmann & Taylor of Montgomery, Ala., were military outfitters, and importers, and their name is frequently found on Confederate buttons. They did not make swords.

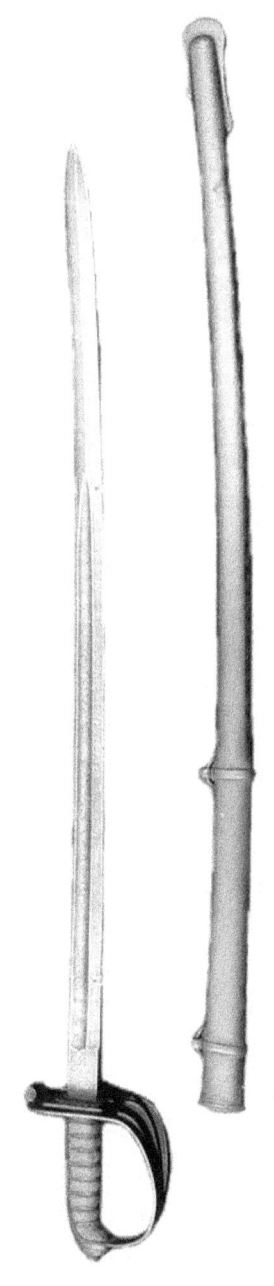

Sabre manufactured by S. Isaac's Campbell, London

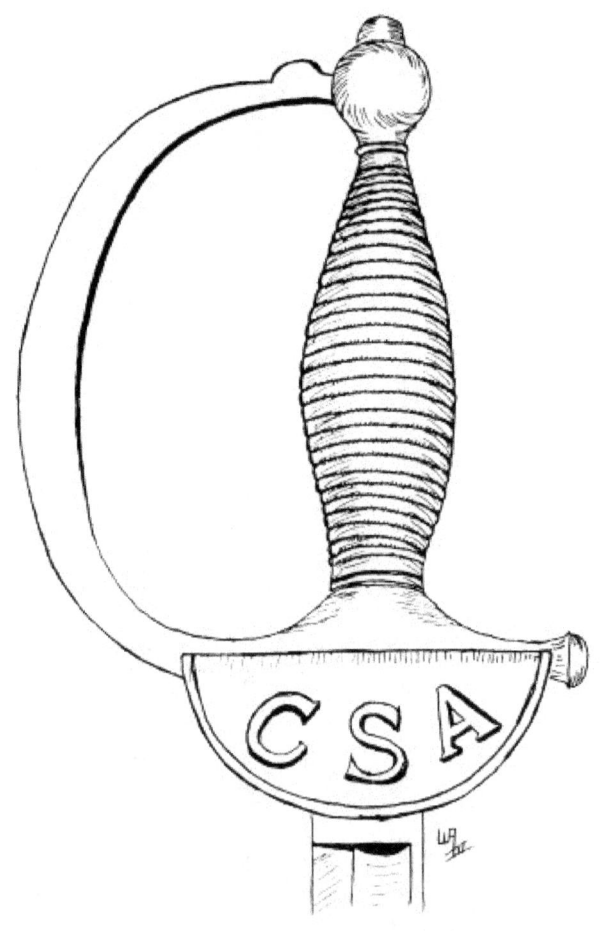

Plate 44

FORTY-FOUR
German-Made Confederate Sword

Pictured is another example of the foreign made Confederate sword.

It is a non-commissioned officer's sword and very well made. Guard and grip are of cast brass. The counter-guard is in the form of a large shield which turns down over the blade on the obverse, and which contains in large raised letters, "C.S.A." The blade is 32 inches long, 7/8 inch wide, and with an over-all length of 38 1/4 inches.

The blade is marked "W. Walsoneid, Solingen."

The sword of this type in the Battle Abbey, came from the collection of the late Gen. Bennett H. Young, of Kentucky.

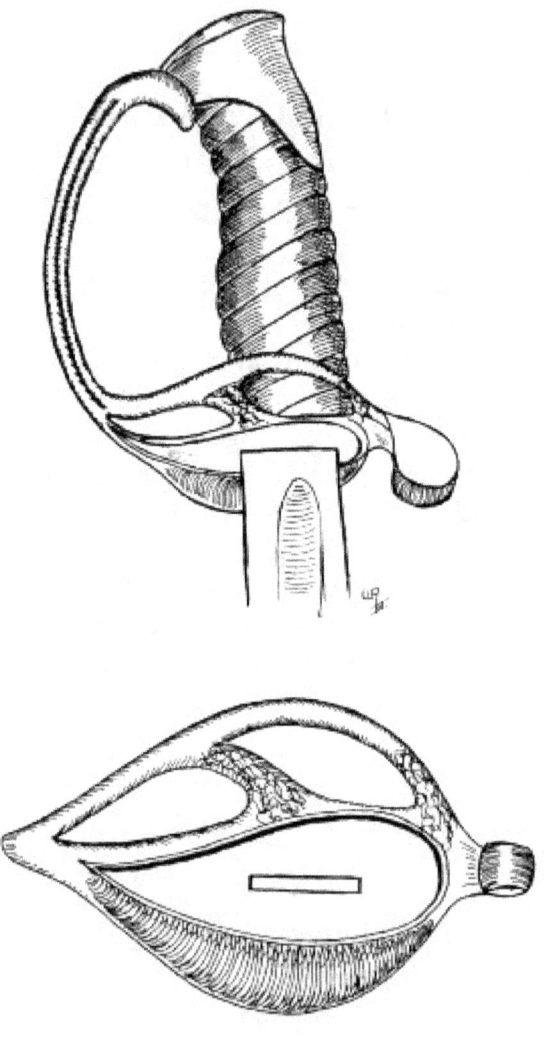

Plate 45

FORTY-FIVE
Unmarked Confederate Officer's Sword

This is a very poor imitation of the U.S. regulation foot officer's sword of the Civil War period, and obviously Confederate. The guard is roughly cast of brass, with an attempt at decoration on the branches. The hilt is of black leather wound with double stranded brass wire. The blade is almost straight, 30 inches long, 1 inch wide, with shallow blood gutter on either side. The number "51" is stamped on the underside of the guard, on the pommel and on the tang of the blade. The scabbard is of leather with brass mounts.

A sword of this type can be seen in the Virginia Room of the Confederate Museum in Richmond, Va.

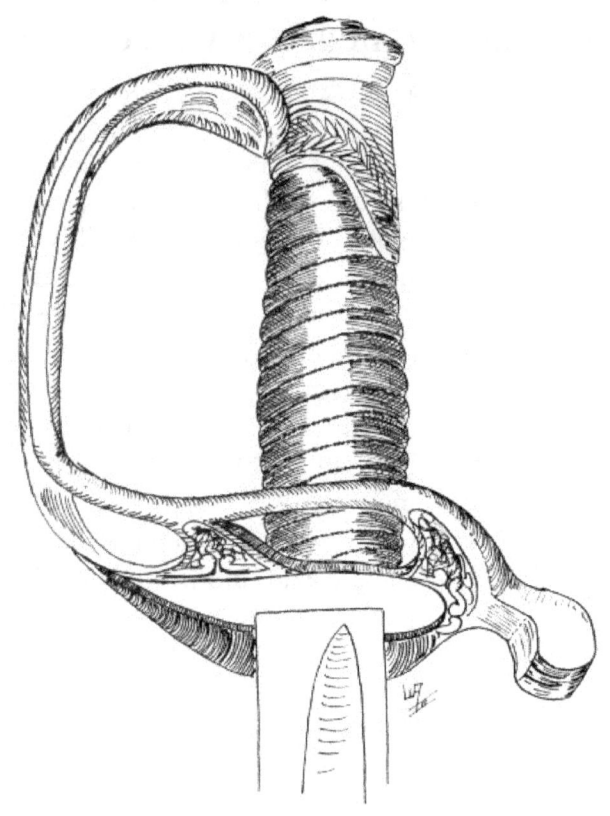

Plate 46

FORTY-SIX
Unmarked Confederate Officer's Sword

A sword very similar to the one just preceding is this crude copy of the U.S. foot officer's sword.

The blade is 31 1/2 inches long, almost straight, 1 1/16 inches wide, with tapering blood gutter on both sides. The guard is poorly cast, and the attempt at decoration on the branches, and pommel are almost indistinquishable. Open spaces have been left in the counterguard instead of the customary rose design. The grip is covered with leather and wound with fourteen turns of double stranded brass wire.

The piece is totally without markings.

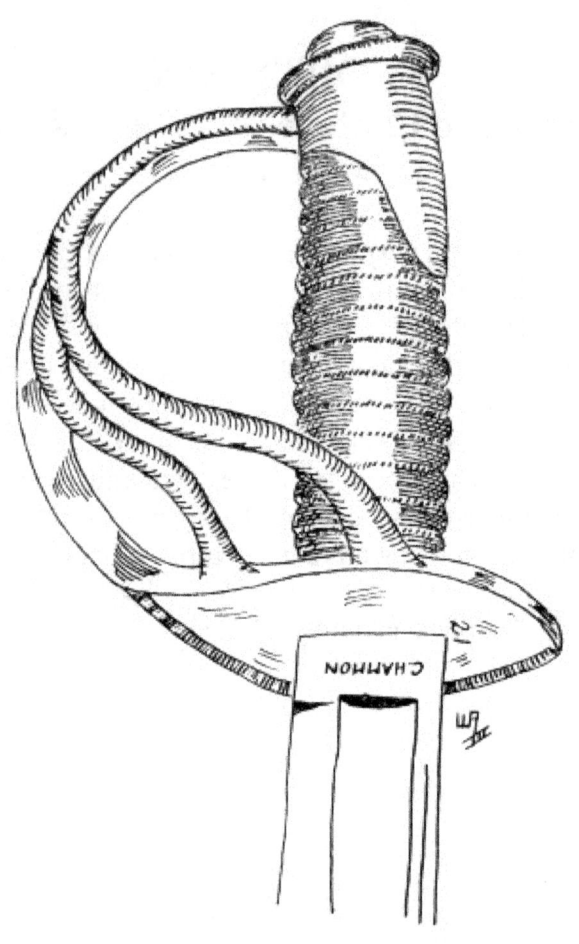

Plate 47

FORTY-SEVEN
Confederate Cavalry Sabre

This sabre is stamped on the blade "C. Hammon." The name is not a familiar one, and I have never heard of a U.S. swordmaker by this name, and so it has been grouped as a possible Confederate.

The sword closely imitates the U.S. Ames model of three branches. Blade is long and curved, with stopped blood gutter. The guard is of cast brass. The grip is covered with leather and wound with double stranded brass wire. The number "21" is stamped on the underside of the guard.

The scabbard is of metal, with metal ring mounts and rings. The scabbard is rather crude, and has been bronze welded.

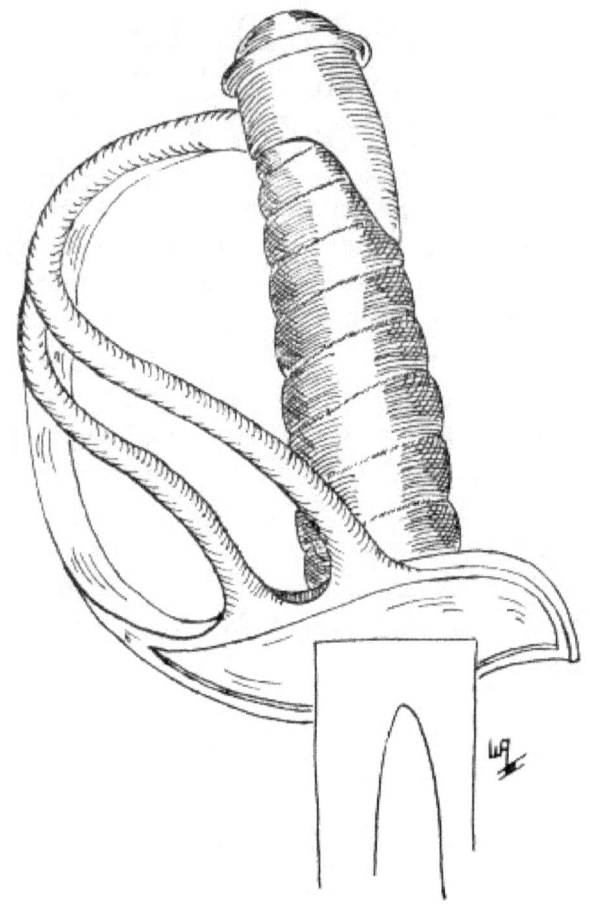

Plate 48

FORTY-EIGHT
Unmarked Confederate Sabre

This is a cavalry sabre of obvious Confederate manufacture, and an imitation of standard U.S. cavalry sabres of this period. The hilt is rather crudely cast brass. The grip is covered with leather and wound with eleven turns of double stranded brass wire. The blade is 34 3/4 inches in length, 1 3/16 inches wide, and over-all length is 40 inches. Blade is rounded on the back, and has a wide shallow groove on either side.

The scabbard is typically Confederate, metal, with brass ring mounts.

A number of obviously Confederate sabres, which more or less conform to the three-branched U.S. Ames model of the Civil War period were made throughout the South during the war. The majority of them are unmarked, and at this date it can be only conjecture as to where they were made, or who made them. Some of the known swordmakers, and whose names do not otherwise appear in this booklet, were: McKennie & Co. of Charlottesville, Va., and T. D. Driscoll of Howardsville, Va. The first, according to *Debow's Review* of March-April, 1862, was turning out six swords a week; and the latter was turning out twenty-eight swords a week.

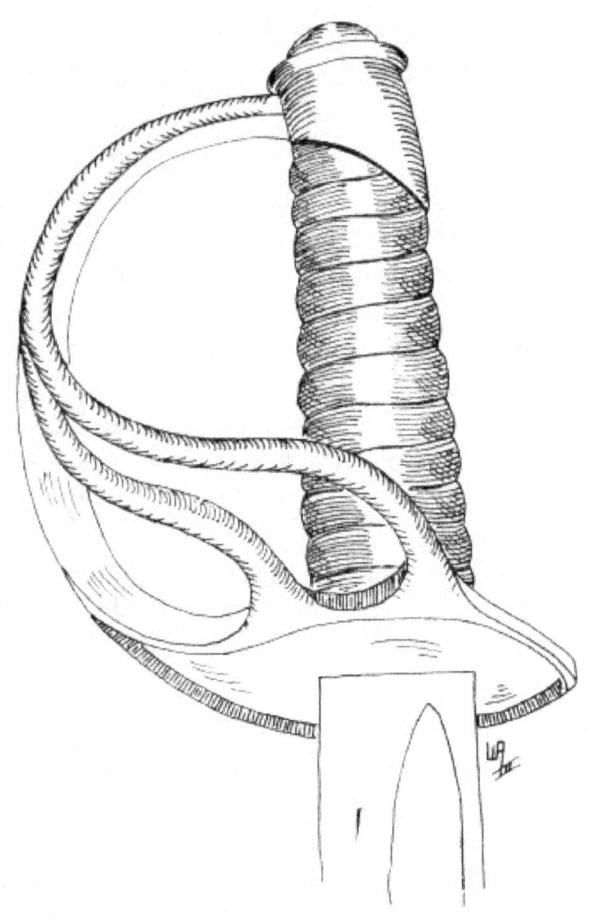

Plate 49

FORTY-NINE
Unmarked Confederate Sabre

This is another unmarked cavalry sabre, of Confederate manufacture, and modeled after those of U.S. Regulation.

Comparison with the one just preceding shows a great similarity, the only difference lying in the shape of the knuckle guard where it joins the hilt.

The blade is 35 inches long, 1 3/16 inches wide, with a wide shallow blood groove on either side. The grip is covered with leather, and wound with single stranded iron wire.

The piece is unmarked. The blade has a flat back.

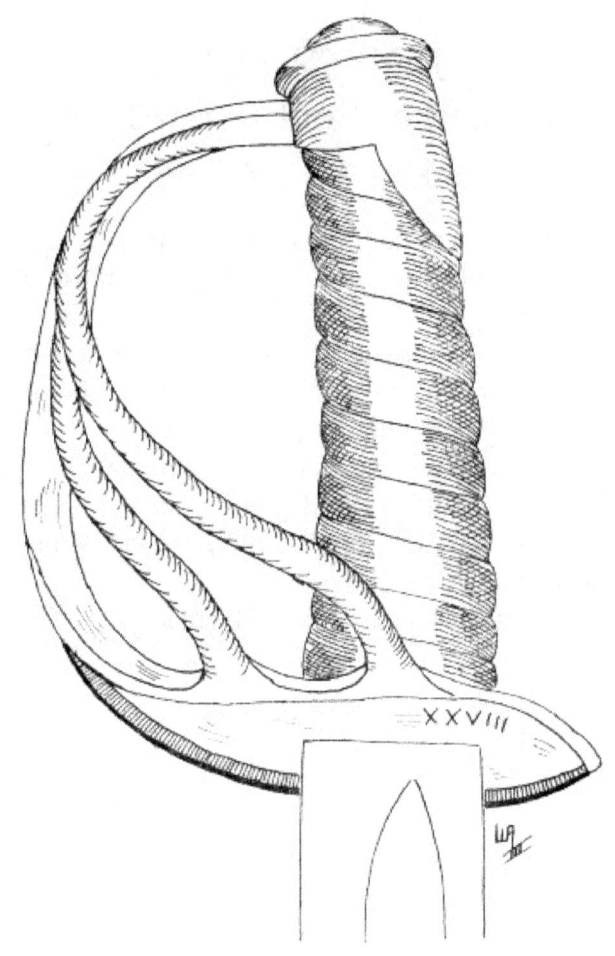

Plate 50

FIFTY
Unmarked Confederate Sabre

This sabre is very similar to the two just preceding, but shows a slight difference in the pommel, and in the knuckle guard where it joins the pommel.

It conforms to the regulation U.S. Cavalry sabre of this period, and is a better-than-average Confederate imitation.

The grip is of brown leather wound with single stranded iron wire. The Roman numerals "XXVIII" are cut in the underside of the guard, these being the only apparent markings.

The blade is curved, 35 inches long, 1 3/16 inches wide, with rounded back, and has a wide shallow blood groove on either side.

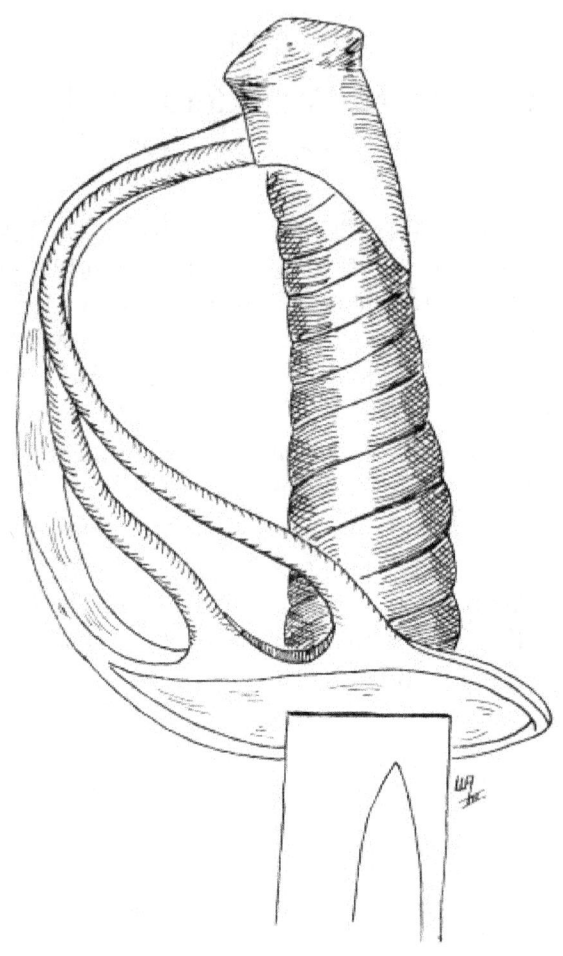

Plate 51

FIFTY-ONE
Unmarked Confederate Sabre

While this sabre is very similar to those preceding, the accompanying sketch shows the crudeness of the pommel.

The grip is of leather wound with ten turns of single stranded copper wire. The blade is 35 1/2 inches long, 1 3/16 inches wide, with tapering blood gutter on either side. Back of the blade is rounded. Over-all length 41 1/2 inches. Weapon appears to be unmarked.

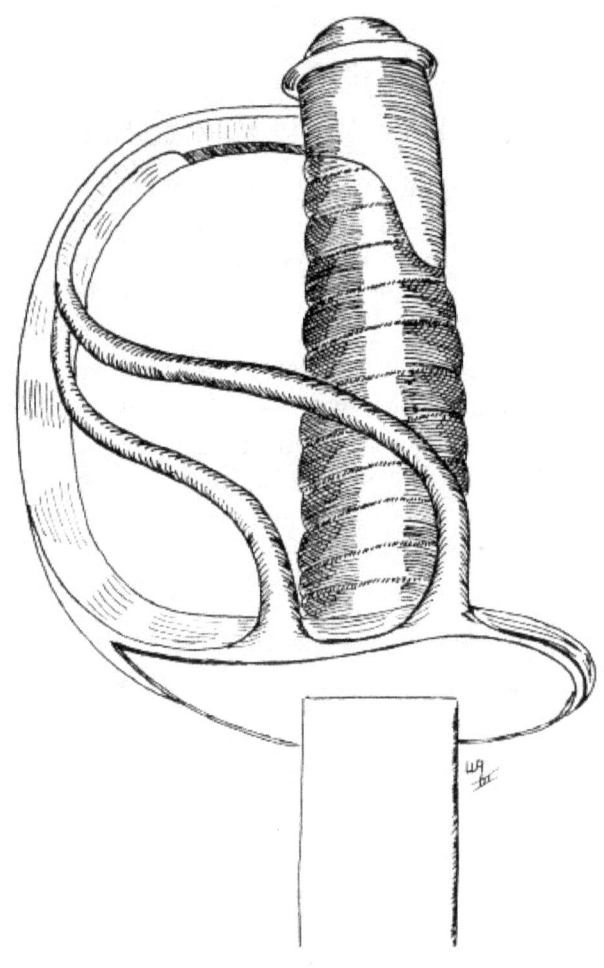

Plate 52

FIFTY-TWO
Unmarked Confederate Sabre

Here is another imitation of the U.S. cavalry sabre of the Civil War period, conforming in general to its Federal counterpart, but lacking grace. The blade is 33 1/2 inches long with rounded back, and without any blood gutter. The guard is of the three-branch variety, but is poorly cast, as is the pommel. The grip is covered with black leather and wound with fourteen turns of double stranded brass wire. Over-all length 39 inches. No marks of identification appear.

The scabbard is typically Confederate, being of metal with two brass ring mounts, the whole being very crude.

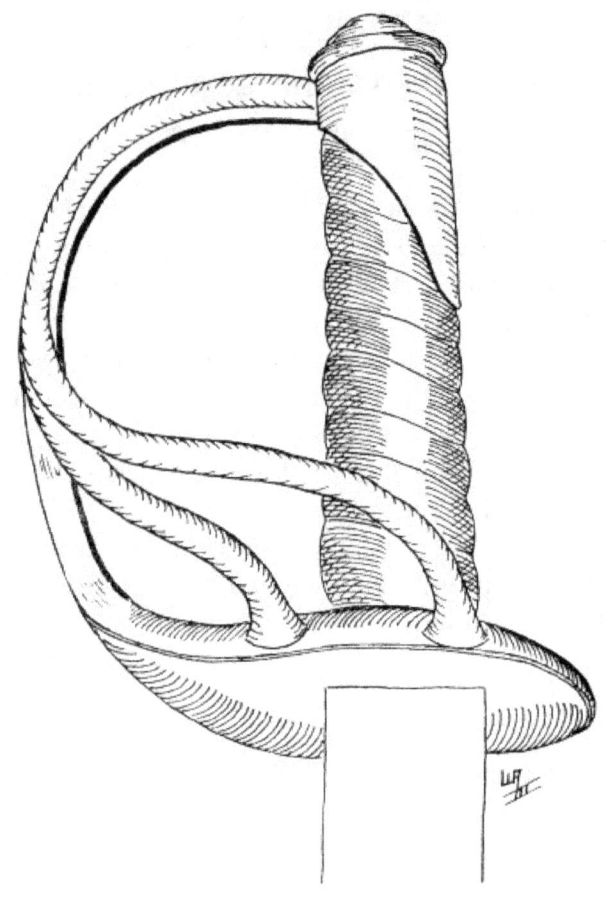

Plate 53

FIFTY-THREE
Unmarked Confederate Sabre

Here is another Confederate-made imitation of the three-branched U.S. cavalry sabre of the Civil War, although poorly made.

The grip is covered with oilcloth, and wound with single stranded iron wire.

The blade is very curved, 34 inches in length, 1 1/4 inches wide, and made without any blood gutter. Back of the blade is flat.

It is possible that this weapon was made by Boyle Gamble & MacFee of Richmond, Va.

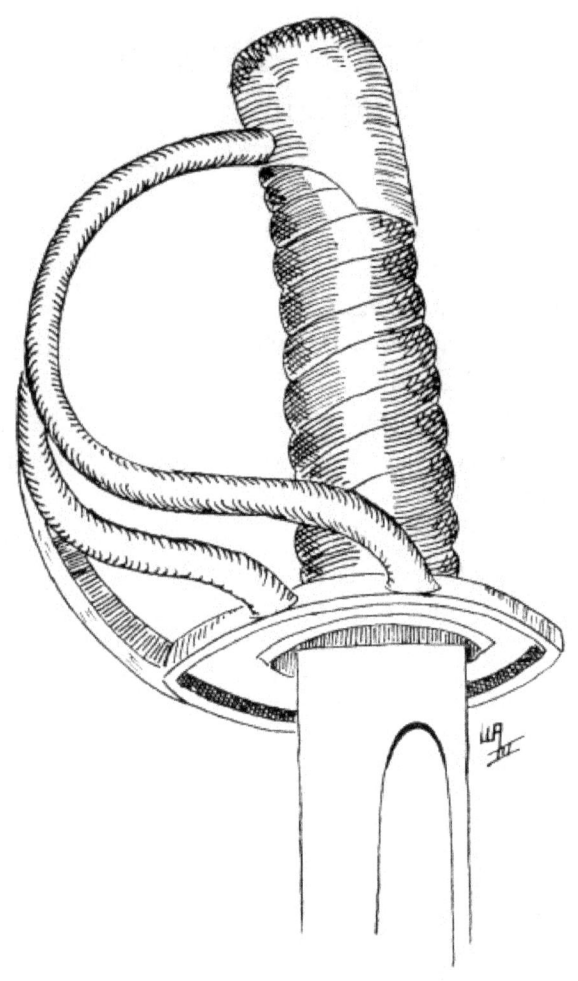

Plate 54

FIFTY-FOUR
Unmarked Confederate Sabre

This cumbersome weapon is of obvious Confederate manufacture, of the three-branch model. The sketch shows the heaviness of the branches, and the entire piece is crude and unfinished in appearance. The Roman numerals "XXII" are cut into the reverse side of the counterguard, and these are the only marks which appear on the weapon.

The blade is 35 1/4 inches long, 1 3/16 inches wide, with a 40 3/4 inches overall. Blade has a tapering shallow blood gutter on either side, and has a rounded back. The grip is covered with leather, and wound with twelve turns of single stranded iron wire. Note the unusual pommel.

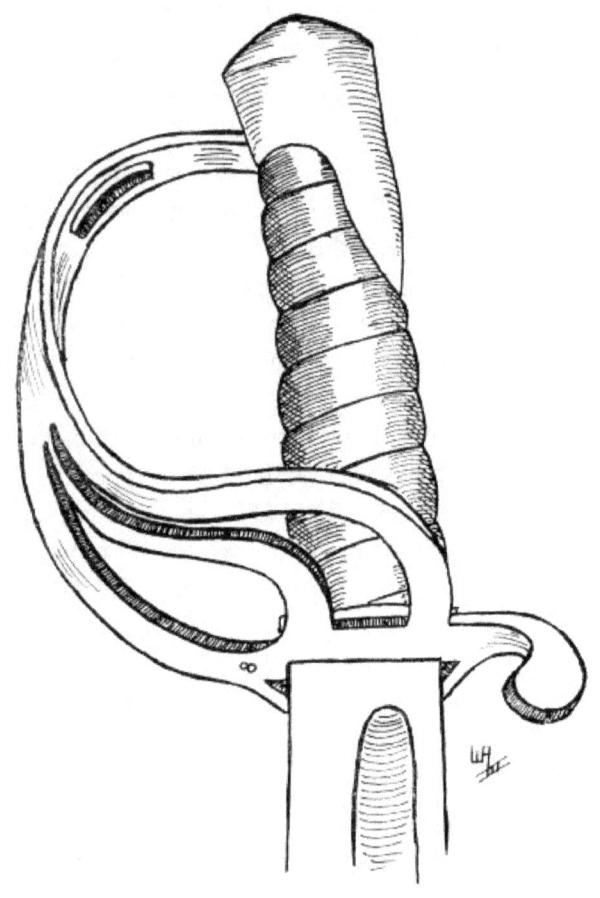

Plate 55

FIFTY-FIVE
Unmarked Confederate Cavalry Sabre
☆ ☆ ☆ ☆

This is a crude copy of the three-branch regulation U.S. Cavalry sabre of the Civil War period, and is of obvious Confederate manufacture.

The guard gives the appearance of having been stamped from a flat piece of sheet brass, but was actually cast. The branches are flat, and the knuckle guard contains a slot for sabre-tasche. The grip is covered with leather and wound with nine turns of heavy single strand iron wire. The number "8" is stamped on the underside of the guard. The pommel is very heavy, and of an inverted cone design, undecorated. The blade is 35 inches long, 1 3/16 inches wide with an almost flat back. A shallow blood gutter runs on either side of the blade, which is curved. The scabbard is crudely made with brass ring mounts, and brass throat.

These sabres appear fairly common, and I have had a half a dozen or so. One I recall had a grip, which apparently had never been covered with leather, but which was wound with single stranded iron wire which followed a line cut into the wood grip.

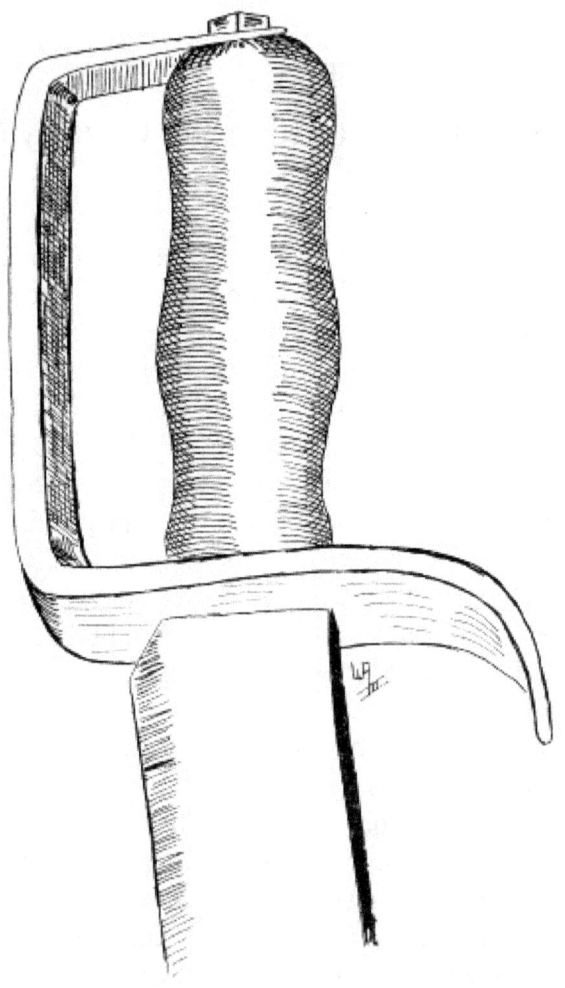

Plate 56

FIFTY-SIX
Home-Made Confederate Sword

An exceptionally crude sword, which must have been made by some local blacksmith, is in the North Carolina Room of the Confederate Museum in Richmond. This sword was carried by Capt. Richard Gatlin, of the Edgecombe Guards of North Carolina.

The weapon has an unusually heavy blade, 21 1/2 inches long, 1 3/4 inches wide, and 1/4 inch thick. The blade evidently was intended to be straight but is affixed to the hilt at a backward angle. The blade has a bowie type point. The guard is of wrought iron, very heavy and crude. The grip is of wood, roughly turned. The guard is fastened to the tang of the blade by an iron nut. The scabbard is of wood covered with thick leather.

The entire sword presents a most ungainly appearance, but as a cut and thrust weapon, must have been deadly.

There is no clue as to the maker.

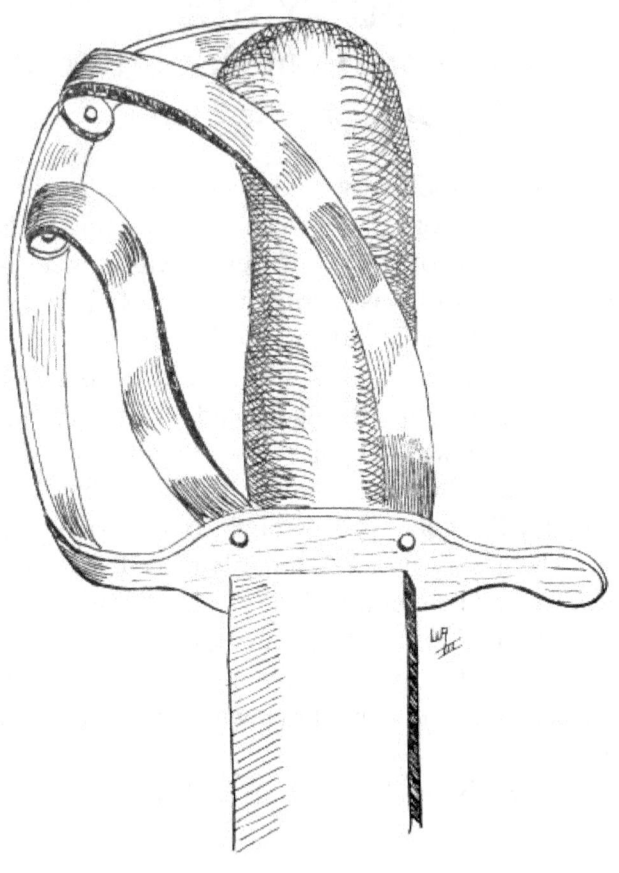

Plate 57

FIFTY-SEVEN
"Home-Made" Confederate Officer's Sword

This "home-made" type officer's sword is obviously of Confederate manufacture. The blade is almost straight, 26 1/2 inches long, 1/8 inches wide, and without blood gutter. The guard is a wrought iron strap to which two additional wrought iron branches have been riveted. The grip is of wood, and has never been covered with leather, or wound with wire. Over-all length is 32 inches. The scabbard is of wood, painted black. It has two copper ring mounts superimposed on tin mounts, and also has a tin toe.

The whole represents a very clumsy appearing weapon.

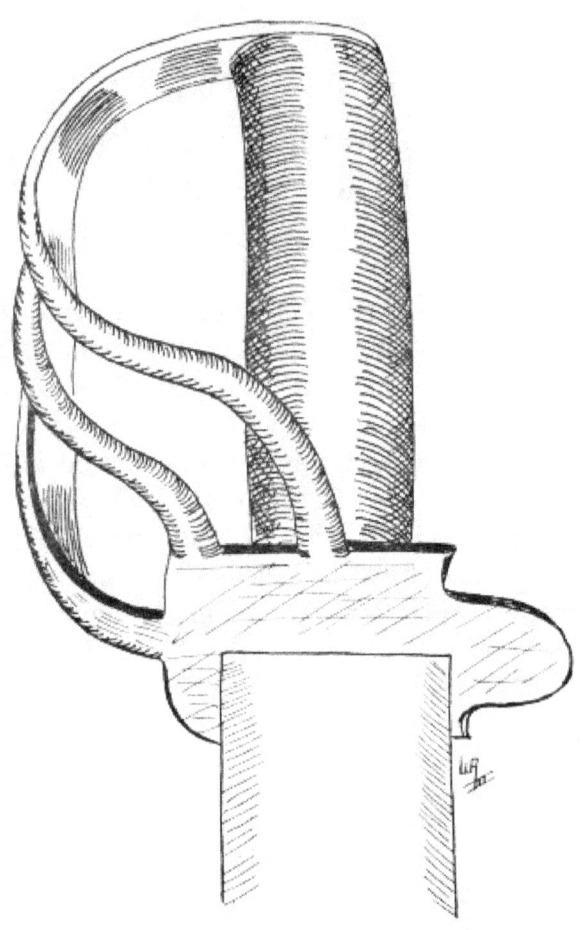

Plate 58

FIFTY-EIGHT
Confederate Naval Cutlass

A very crude pair of Confederate naval cutlasses hang in the Confederate Museum in Richmond, Va. The pair formed a part of the armament of the Confederate States Letter of Marque Privateer *Jeff Davis*, which sailed from Charleston, S.C., June 28th, 1861, and cruised off the Atlantic coast, making seven captures before she was wrecked on the St. Augustine Bar, off the Florida coast in August, 1861.

The swords have heavy double-edged blades, 2 1/2 inches wide, 22 inches long. The grip is of wood, and the guard of wrought iron of the three-branched variety. The weapons are every bit as clumsy as the picture makes them appear.

They are without markings.

Farmount

FIFTY-NINE
Swords of Confederate Manufacture in the National Museum and Described in U.S. National Museum Bulletin No. 163, by Theodore T. Belate

There are various Confederate-made swords in the National Museum in Washington, D.C. I have included here only those swords which have not been described elsewhere in this booklet.

A foot officer's sword with a heavy slightly curved blade 81.5 cm long, 3 cm wide. Blade contains a tapering blood gutter on either side. The grip, pommel, and guard are all of the regulation type, but crudely made. The reverse side of the counterguard bears the letters "C.S." in large capitals. This sword belongs to the Alfred E. Hopkins collection, and has an over-all length of 96 cm. (Plate No. 23, fig. No. 2).

Another sword of the foot officer's type, has an unusually large guard, the front of which bears a pelican on her nest between the letters "C.S." in large capitals. Over-all length 91 cm., with a blade 77.5 cm. long, 2.9 wide. The blade is marked "Dufilno, N. Orleans" (Plate No. 23, fig. No. 3).

An artillery officer's sabre in the National Museum, and said to be of great beauty, conforms to the U.S. artillery sabre of the same period. The blade is etched with a variety of fruit and floral designs, and the reverse shows a trophy of Confederate flags above crossed cannon, floral and oak leaf designs and a scroll inscribed "C.S." The grip is of leather, wound in grooves with ten turns of gilt wire. The guard and pommel conform to the U.S. The scabbard is of steel with three brass mounts. Length 90.2 cm., blade 76.4 cm., 3 cm. wide (Plate No. 22, fig. No. 3).

A Confederate Cavalry officer's sabre has a long slightly curved blade with quill back. Both sides of the blade are decorated with floral designs in silver chasing, a trophy, and a five-pointed star with the letters of the word "T-E-X-A-S" between the points. The grip is of wood with twelve parallel vertical grooves, and the whole is surmounted by a plain brass strip terminating in a plain circular pommel. The knuckle-guard is a plain brass strip with three branches uniting on the obverse with a narrow oval counterguard. Length 100.5 cm., blade 87.2 cm., 3 cm. wide (Plate No. 23, fig. No. 5).

SIXTY
Swords Stamped "C.S.A."

Much could be written on the subject of Confederate items which are identifiable as Confederate only by a stamped "CSA," or by a stamped "Va" for Virginia, or "Ala" for Alabama, and so forth. Unquestionably a large number of such items are genuine, and were stamped either at the time of manufacture, or at the time of repair by the Confederate Ordnance to distinguish Government property from that which belonged to various States. The same applies to items which were marked with the State's name or initials to distinguish it from Confederate States property. I have seen a number of swords so marked, and because of the low price, in some instances, or because of the method of acquiring, made me feel reasonably sure that they were genuine.

On the other hand, a set of metal stamping tools are inexpensive, and as the price of a Confederate sword or gun is always higher than the corresponding U.S., or foreign weapon, the incentive for an unscrupulous dealer or collector to stamp "CSA," is not slight. Unfortunately there is no way to tell the sword which was repaired by the Confederate Government, and which was stamped by them "CSA," from the one which was French to begin with, and which was turned into a genuine (?) Confederate last week by a dishonest enthusiast plus a set of metal stamps.

Where possible I have always avoided any piece which can be called Confederate only because of a stamped marking, and where without the stamp it would be called U.S., or French, etc.

www.ingramcontent.com/pod-product-compliance
Lightning Source LLC
LaVergne TN
LVHW051059080426
835508LV00019B/1959